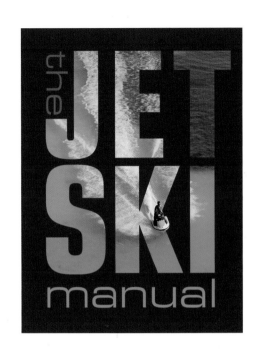

the JET SKI manual

the JET SKI

Christophe Harmand

manual

ADLARD COLES NAUTICAL · LONDON

Published by Adlard Coles Nautical
an imprint of Bloomsbury Publishing Plc
50 Bedford Square, London WC1B 3DP
www.adlardcoles.com

First published in French (as *Jet & Scooter Mer & Rivière*)
by E-T-A-I in 2009.

© E-T-A-I 2009

E-T-A-I
Antony Parc 2
10 Place du Général de Gaulle
92160 ANTONY
France

ISBN 978-1-4081-5281-2

A CIP catalogue record for this book is available from the British
Library.

This book is produced using paper that is made from wood grown
in managed, sustainable forests. It is natural, renewable and
recyclable. The logging and manufacturing processes conform to the
environmental regulations of the country of origin.

Design by Austin Taylor
Page layouts by Susan McIntyre
Typeset in 10.75 on 15pt GriffithGothic light

Printed and bound in Croatia by Zrinski

Note: while all reasonable care has been taken in the publication of this
book, the publisher takes no responsibility for the use of the methods
or products described in the book.

Contents

Preface

JET SKIING is one of the most exciting motor sports and as the discipline continues to evolve, so too will the thrills and pleasure it brings.

Twenty years ago, a stand-up jet ski was more like a dirt bike. Today, the top machines reach 150km/h on the water and riding them far outweighs the pleasures offered by any race car.

I began jet skiing in Marseille at the end of the 80s to stop hurting myself in motocross racing! Today, after 15 world titles, I may just have discovered the recipe for success. You have to work constantly to improve your performance and be prepared to make technical improvements to your jet ski. But the most important thing – the real secret – is to be surrounded and supported by a great team, and I'd like to take this opportunity to thank those who have always helped and advised me: my family – my father in particular – and also Yves Van Heers, with whom I won my first world championship title against the US in 1991.

Whether you are a seasoned jet skier or a novice, I would recommend that you are always open to good advice, of which there is plenty within this book.

*Nicolas **Rius***

15 WORLD CHAMPIONSHIP TITLES
15 EUROPEAN CHAMPIONSHIP TITLES
7 FRENCH CHAMPIONSHIP TITLES
5 US CHAMPIONSHIP TITLES

Holder of 15 world titles, Nicolas Rius is one of jet skiing's iconic champions.

Today the world market is largely dominated by three-seater machines used mainly for recreation.

The use of jet skis in the UK is regulated mainly by local by-laws.

Introduction

RIDING A JET SKI is a wonderful recreational activity that sits somewhere between motor boating and motorcycling. The original idea sprang from a desire to translate the feeling of riding on two wheels to the aquatic environment, and today this has certainly been achieved. Jet skiing has evolved into a pastime that reaches beyond its original market, with families and a wide range of age groups finding great pleasure in the adventure it brings.

I started jet skiing at the beginning of the 90s. At that time, the jet ski, which had a bad reputation – generally for good reasons – was reserved for experts. Today, the reverse is true. Operating a jet ski is simple, thanks to well-established rules and machines that are easy to use. The rules may at first appear restrictive to novices, who are usually not well informed when they are just starting out. This guide is designed to highlight key issues along the way and to provide simple and helpful answers. I have also tried to include more detailed technical information for experienced riders so that they can add to their body of knowledge.

After two decades on the water, I still remember the arrival of the first jet ski magazine on the news-stands, which included coverage of tests carried out around Paris in the middle of winter, as well as reports of the victories of French riders competing at the highest world level in the American desert. But the best moments on a jet ski are still those when you find yourself in tune with nature – with the sea, the waves and their inhabitants, like the dolphins that came to play for ten minutes around our hulls while we ran at full speed during a trip around Mont Saint-Michel, or the shoal of flying fish we encountered in the warm waters of the Caribbean...

*Christophe **Harmand***

1
HISTORY

A young sport

THE HISTORY OF JET SKIING does not date back very far. It began in the 1970s in the United States, where so many mechanised sports were born. Bombardier was the first manufacturer to market a 'marine motorcycle', the Sea-Doo, in 1968. Later, Kawasaki would develop and manufacture the very first jet ski. While the name 'Jet Ski' is a registered trademark belonging to Kawasaki, the term has since been adopted into everyday usage.

In 1973, 'jet ski' referred to the stand-up model with an articulated arm. But to really understand the jet ski's origins, we need to go back to the world of mechanised sport in the 1960s.

↑ *In 1990, Kawasaki produced the ultimate version of its stand-up model with a 550cc engine*

→ *Kawasaki launches its first Jet Ski in the US in 1973, thereby inventing a completely new sport*

An American inventor

AFTER SEVERAL UNCONVINCING home-built projects in the US, which were closer to a single- or two-seater motorised canoe than a jet ski, Clayton Jacobson, a bank clerk and dirt bike enthusiast from Arizona, dreamed of a way of transferring the feeling of driving a two-wheeled motor vehicle to the aquatic environment. In 1965, he quit his job to devote himself full-time to this project. His first prototype had an aluminium hull and a jet propulsion system – a jet pump – rather than a traditional propeller. His concept was a cross between a motorbike and a water ski – clearly the source of the term 'jet ski'. For his use of jet propulsion, he is recognised today as the inventor of the jet ski.

The first jet ski fails

↓ The first marine motorcycle was a failure, mainly due to reliability issues. Sales quickly came to a halt.

THE FIRST MANUFACTURER to be interested in his work was Bombardier, maker of the Ski-Doo snowmobile, and then the Sea-Doo range in 1967. In 1968, the collaboration between the inventor and the manufacturer resulted in the 320, a small watercraft with a seat, a handlebar and a round rather than a V hull – but with a jet pump. Because

← In 1968,
Bombardier sold
the first marine
motorcycle using
the Jacobson
patent. This was
the very first mass-
produced jet ski on
the market

of these features, the 320 is today regarded as the first true jet ski runabout. The term 'sit-down' is also used for runabout jet skis.

The advertising of the day promised that you would be able to 'play like a dolphin'. But in truth, due to inadequate development, the machine was not easy to control and was essentially an after-sales disaster with multiple technical problems, most notably a lack of waterproofing. It should also be noted that the 18hp Rotax engine was air-cooled! Basically, it was a failure and production stopped in 1970, even though the exclusive licensing rights ran until 1971.

Kawasaki manufactures its first 'Jet Ski'

BEFORE KNOCKING AT KAWASAKI'S DOOR, Jacobson went back to the drawing board while waiting for his contract with Bombardier to expire. Once again, his new design used the idea of jet propulsion. This time, however, the machine was much more compact and had a single seat – which was positioned over the engine hatch – and the arm was fixed. Although incomplete, the design was more fully developed. The first prototype had an aluminium hull, but this was soon replaced with a fibreglass one. Legend has it that six prototypes were made before Kawasaki took over the project development and finalised it, making the arm supporting the handlebar mobile so that the pilot could position himself better on the machine. Japanese companies, particularly motorbike manufacturers, have revolutionised the world of two-wheeled leisure and travel, overshadowing European-made machines with unrivalled technological advances. Honda, with its formidable CB750 Four, changed history forever with a mass-produced motorcycle that had a four-stroke engine, four cylinders and a front disc brake. This Japanese dominance of the market is due in part to their practice of seeking out good ideas wherever they can find them, particularly in the United States. So by the end of the 1960s, the large Japanese motorcycle manufacturers had American research and development departments staffed with American personnel tasked with designing products their compatriots wanted. There are many examples of the success of this approach – the invention of the all-terrain or 'trail' motorbike by Yamaha in collaboration with its Californian project leaders was an American one, and the invention at Honda of the ATV (the three-wheeled ancestor of the quad bike) was another. Allowing an American inventor to design a 'marine motorcycle' resulted in the jet ski – the third notable success of the Japanese approach towards development.

The first Kawasaki Jet Skis were almost handmade, with provisions in the initial design for a fixed, raised arm.

Sadly, the story also has a sour note: an intense legal battle between Kawasaki and Jacobson began in 1976 and continued until 1992. Kawasaki Motors Corporation USA finally acknowledged that Jacobson was indeed the inventor of the Jet Ski – an admission that saved the company $20 million in damages and interest. Even though Kawasaki withdrew its claim of ownership of the original idea for the jet ski, the company did develop the design on an industrial and cultural scale. Kawasaki is undeniably responsible for the Jet Ski's successful technical development, and above all for the popularisation of this new nautical motorised sport.

A new start

THE FIRST KAWASAKI JET SKI was marketed in the United States in 1973. It had a twin-cylinder, two-stroke, water-cooled engine and was manoeuvrable thanks to a handlebar that made the jet flow move to the right or left. In addition to the safety provided by the use of a jet pump, Kawasaki's first Jet Ski had two other safety features in case the driver fell off: a self-righting system that automatically set the machine back on its waterline; and autorotation, which meant the Jet Ski would idle and go around in circles to enable recovery by the dislodged rider. The design of the first Jet Ski was now complete and it was the first real marine motorcycle. Green in colour, this very first Jet Ski was available with a flat (WSAA) or V-shaped (WSAB) hull. However, its marketing and production remained relatively limited.

↓ With the '440', which referred to its engine capacity, Kawasaki began mass production of its Jet Ski, leading to widespread adoption of its formula.

In 1976, Kawasaki started mass production of this prototype. Now called the JS400, improved and white in colour, the Jet Ski was manufactured primarily in the United States at Kawasaki's factory in Lincoln, Nebraska. It was the first Japanese product to be mass-produced on American soil. Improved again in 1977 with a 440cc engine, and once more in 1985 with a 550cc engine, the first Kawasaki Jet Skis were made until 1998, the last 300 units being sold exclusively in Japan.

↓ In 1986, Kawasaki, inventor of the stand-up Jet Ski, marketed its first sit-down Jet Ski which with its front apron and flat floor resembled a scooter. Thus, the TS (Tandem Sport) launched the 'sea scooter' fad.

In 1986, the Sea-Doo returned to the jet ski market with the 'XP'. This high-performance and reliable machine was an immediate success.

The Jet Ski gains acceptance

With strong marketing from Kawasaki, the period 1976–1977 was marked by increased acceptance of the Jet Ski, as well as of other concepts, such as the 'wetbike' – a real motorbike mounted on skis, also propelled by a jet pump. The machine is famous for its appearance in the James Bond movie *The Spy Who Loved Me*. Until the middle of the 1980s, jet skiing was not seen as a form of recreation, as it is today, but was perceived simply as a sport, like skiing, with a strong American stamp. With the arrival of sit-down jet skis in the second half of the 1980s, the jet ski world really exploded. In 1986, Bombardier returned the Sea-Doo to the market with an ultra-modern and reliable machine. Kawasaki also marketed its first sit-down Jet Ski, and Yamaha, already known in the nautical world for its outboard motors, also entered the sit-down as well as the stand-up jet ski markets with its first SuperJet. With this new offering, the market became truly competitive. Initially reserved for sportsmen, the jet ski was now easier to handle and control – a formula

↓ With the X2, Kawasaki debuted a strange new jet ski concept without an articulated handlebar, or seat. Although aesthetically odd, the X2 was formidably efficient on closed-course circuits.

↑ In 1987, Kawasaki marketed a brand-new stand-up jet ski with a big 650cc engine, marking the beginning of the evolution of stand-up jet skis.

WITH SUPERCHARGERS, FLAPS, TRIM SYSTEMS, HYDRAULIC SUSPENSION AND BRAKES, MODERN JET SKIS MAKE USE OF ALL THE LATEST TECHNOLOGY.

that quickly made it accessible to a wider user base. Although intimidating in its infancy, the jet ski now had universal appeal and the market was quickly shaped by competition between the three brands. This important change opened jet skiing to the general public and it became a family leisure activity to rival other activities in the boating world. From this moment on, the single-rider jet ski with an articulated arm was marginalised and became almost the exclusive province of enthusiasts and sportsmen, with its devotees being generally young and from the world of motorbikes.

The US market connection

THE JET SKI MARKET really exploded in the early 1990s with the arrival of sit-down machines. Jet ski country is still the United States – nearly all jet skis are manufactured there, even the Japanese brands – and as the jet ski's most important market, new products are designed to

↓ In the search for new concepts, the Kawasaki SC has gone down in history as the first jet ski offering two side-by-side seats. Note that while under way it was possible to move the handlebar to the left or right.

↑ In 1995, with its 900cc engine, Kawasaki's ZXI marked a big step forward in jet ski development for power as well as engine size.

meet American needs and desires. To put things into perspective, in 2007 the US market was estimated at over 65,000 units, while in France, for example, 3,200 new machines were sold. So the United States remains the primary jet ski market and has brands and products which are not exported to other countries. An example of this is Honda, which reserves its jet skis exclusively for the US market.

The technical revolution of the 21st Century

AT THE BEGINNING of this century, the jet ski world underwent a significant technical revolution. The two-stroke engine, simple and light – but polluting – was now in the legislative hot seat and adoption of the more modern four-stroke engine became mandatory. This change to an engine with valves caused significant modifications to the machines, particularly to their weight. Heavier and much more complex, modern jet skis are intricate works of engineering approaching the level of race boats. With superchargers, flaps, trim systems, hydraulic suspension and brakes, modern jet skis make use of all the latest technology. Jet ski manufacturers deserve recognition for the speed with which they successfully changed over to the four-stroke engine, while maintaining performance and reliability. However, the maintenance needed by these small engineering masterpieces is considerable.

↓ *Yamaha marketed its first 'marine jets' in 1986 with the 650T and 650TL, two simple, robust and very easy-to-manoeuvre jet skis.*

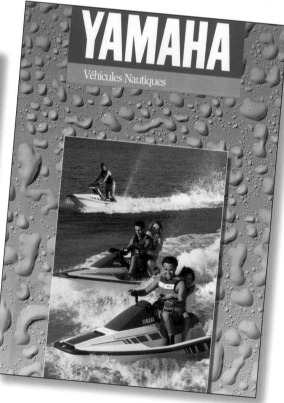

→ *In 1987, Yamaha competed directly with Kawasaki with its first stand-up jet ski. The SuperJet is still in the Japanese company's catalogue today but has been modernised considerably.*

↓ *Yamaha's WaveBlaster is a true water motorcycle – very entertaining to ride in all settings*

2
BUYER'S
GUIDE

GIVEN THE HIGH PRICE of new jet skis, careful consideration is required to help you find one that meets both your budget and intended use. You need to ask yourself the right questions and establish exactly what you are looking for. This really comes down to: identifying where you will be riding (open water, inland waterways, river), what you will be using your jet ski for (touring, closed course, playing with towables with the family, or a little of all three) and how often you will be using it during the year (just for the summer holidays or every weekend of the season, perhaps).

Budgeting for your jet ski

WITH A FIRST-TIME PURCHASE, the price of the machine is not the only consideration. The initial budget should include, notably, the trailer required to transport and launch it, and the riders' equipment, eg wetsuits and lifejackets. In addition to these, your budget has to include running costs and above all fuel, which remains by far the most costly item, then care and maintenance, and possibly storage fees. In addition, your budget must cover insurance – even if this is not mandatory – and eventual launching fees. Operating a jet ski is certainly a costly sport, especially for powerful, open water-going machines. As a guideline, you should count on anything up to £14,000 for a new, three-seater machine and trailer; around £200 for the rider's equipment; and a maintenance budget of approximately £300 for the first year. For a stand-up jet ski, the entry price is approximately £6,000 pounds.

The jet ski market offers different machines for different environments – open water or inland waterways – as well as for different uses, such as sport or recreation.

Used jet skis are also available from dealers, and more recent models usually come with a good deal in terms of warranties and servicing.

Then there is the private used market, which offers few guarantees and should therefore be explored only by those with the experience required to determine a jet ski's true condition.

Categories

NOWADAYS, THE JET SKI MARKET is well established and focuses on three-seater machines. This category accounts for most sales in the UK and has largely overtaken the market for two-seater machines, which are mainly used for competitions. Then there's the stand-up jet ski, which for purists is the 'noblest' design, but the use of which remains limited. A new category is also emerging with the arrival of high-end, unique machines with prices to match, such as the HSR-Benelli from Austria, as well as the FZ950, a handmade stand-up jet ski produced in small numbers in France. The three big jet ski manufacturers also offer luxury models for this market. Apart from the one-, two- and three-seater format, the market is largely divided by the requirements of a machine's intended use, e.g. recreation or sport. Each manufacturer therefore has its own market focus.

The three-seater recreation category

You can have great fun on inland waters with these jet skis but they are particularly well suited to family excursions, especially at sea. The power level of these machines varies between 120 and 160hp, which makes them versatile while still being within the capability of all experience levels. The price differences between the machines in this category are determined by the level of equipment acquired at purchase, and the presence or otherwise of navigational aid systems.

↑ The UK market today is dominated by recreational three-seater jet skis, such as the affordably priced Kawasaki STX.

The three-seater deluxe recreation category

These machines are more powerful, much better equipped and more versatile. With engines of up to 250hp, they offer great comfort and a stable ride at sea. They also allow you to go on a long family ride and easily pull a towable or a waterskier. They are designed primarily for operation at sea.

The three-seater sport category

Machines in this category have engines of up to 250 or 260hp, but with a clearly sporty feel. The maintenance and fuel budgets are generally considerable, but the thrills and especially the speed are there in abundance, with top speeds exceeding 100km/h.

↑ *Manufacturers are competing for increased engine power and offer machines that easily exceed 260hp. These machines are sporty, fuel-hungry and require considerable maintenance.*

→ *Sport jet skis, mainly two-seaters, offer a thrilling driving experience, especially at sea.*

The two-seater sport category

There are now only a few machines in this category, targeted at competitive sports, with engine powers exceeding 250hp. This category is designed primarily for thrill-seekers.

Stand-up jet skis

The stand-up jet ski is by far the most affordable of the machines available and the easiest to operate; it also has the sportiest design and is the least versatile. Riding one requires you to be both in good physical condition and have good technique, but with modern and stable machines that have come a long way from the original ones, the stand-up jet ski is accessible to almost everyone. Because it is a single-seater, you miss out on companionship and conviviality, and sea excursions are effectively out of the question. Nevertheless, these machines do enable us to have fun on inland waterways, even those that are not particularly large. With five or six buoys you can have a closed course on a lake, and you can easily play at sea too. Fun and exciting to ride, the stand-up jet ski allows us to enjoy ourselves at an affordable price, since its maintenance and storage requirements are relatively low.

↑ *Today, the stand-up jet ski is less common. It is targeted for sports use, is cheaper to buy and has lower operating costs.*

Unique machines

The jet ski market now offers some very high-end machines, with the major manufacturers offering models crammed with technology, like the Sea-Doo RXT and the Yamaha FX SHO. Standing alongside these hi-tech flagships are even more exclusive jet skis, such as the HSR-Benelli with its V6 engines, or their stand-up jet ski, which is the only one with a turbocharged four-stroke engine. Since 2009 there has been a French-produced line of high-end jet skis which emerged from the competition with the limited-production FZ950. This stand-up jet ski is made by Frank Zapata, the French 2008 world champion, and is marketed as a real racing machine.

Single-seater sport machines

This category no longer exists today, but some machines are still available on the used market, even though the design never enjoyed real success. The category includes different designs, all of which tried to provide the riding sensation of a stand-up jet ski in a seated configuration. On the whole, these original machines were trying to emulate the water motorcycle concept. The best example of this is still the Kawasaki X2, which was simply a stand-up model with the arm replaced by a handlebar. This design, which enjoyed some success at the end of the 1970s, was updated and relaunched in 2006, then disappeared from the market, despite its efficiency. Sea-Doo also abandoned the idea in 2007, stopping production of its 3D, a modular-arm machine that could be fitted with a seat in a few minutes. The most successful design in this category belonged to Yamaha with its 1995 WaveBlaster 1, which came the closest to being a true marine motorcycle.

↑ *Sea-Doo produces a model designed specifically for towing; a ballast system eliminates wake wash. This system is designed primarily for use with wakeboards.*

Honda produces an efficient jet ski with the AquaTrax turbo exclusively for the American market. This machine is not exported outside the US, where it is made.

Jetboats

Jetboats combine the advantages of a boat with jet propulsion. They can be used as a dinghy on large vessels.

The jetboat, as the name implies, is a cross between a jet ski and a boat. Like jet skis, these ultra-sporty boats are driven by jet pumps and don't have an external propeller. Sea-Doo has a complete range of about 15 models, with power ranging from 155 to 510hp for models with two jets. There are also some jetboats made by boatbuilders, in particular luxury yacht builders, which are designed to serve as a dinghy. The Italian yacht builder Arimar, for example, offers the Sprint Jet, a semi-rigid inflatable with luxury finishing, including a teak deck.

Sea-Doo offers a large range of jetboats, with engines that can exceed 500hp. These high-end, ultra-sporty boats have the advantage of not having an exposed propeller, which gives them an undeniable safety benefit and shallow draft.

Manufacturers' warranties

JET SKIS GENERALLY have a one-year manufacturer's warranty. The warranty is usually limited to normal use and requires that certain conditions are met: for example, that maintenance should be done by an authorised dealer and that the machine must not be modified. A broken engine for a high-power, supercharged machine is expensive and some manufacturers are more fussy than others in applying their warranty. Adhering scrupulously to their warranty terms, some manufacturers systematically refuse to cover a machine that has been modified in any way – even with an impeller or a common accessory. You should follow your dealer's recommendations carefully in this regard. Note that participating in any sports competition automatically voids the manufacturer's warranty.

Buying a used jet ski

THE SECOND-HAND MARKET presents some interesting opportunities and also some seasonal price variations: it is more profitable to buy a jet ski in the autumn and sell it in the spring than vice versa. This explains, at least in part, why some used jet skis can appear to be a particularly good deal. It remains to be seen if they really are.

↓ *Buying a used jet ski from a dealer or private party can save you money.*

First, you need to know what is the 'right' price for the machine. You can get an idea by checking the prices quoted in magazines and on specialist Internet sites. These used-equipment guides generally apply a simple annual discount to the new price: usually 20% for the first year, 15% for the second and 10% for each following year. These rates do not take into account factors such as the value of rental machines at the end of their career, which are not very sought after. On average, jet skis that have been used solely for recreation usually have between 35 and 50 hours of use per year, with a premium or discount applied for anything outside this average. To determine the exact value of a machine, you also have to take into account optional parts and accessories, which are difficult to price. We know that a dealer usually retains 15% of the purchase price of a used machine; on the other hand, he assumes responsibility for it. However, based on the outcome of recent court cases, you should bear in mind that the dealer's responsibility may be limited to providing advice and may not include anything more substantive in the case of litigation.

This stand-up jet ski may have been souped up – at least, it has an air filter that is not original equipment and that requires special adjustment. For reliability, always choose a machine with only original equipment.

Where to find used jet skis

AS A BUYER you have two options when looking to purchase a used jet ski: go to a professional, or go to a private individual. Going down the professional road will mean that you are likely to get a serviced machine in good condition, as well as indispensable advice for getting started. For someone who is inexperienced, buying from a pro is a simple and efficient way to acquire a good used machine. Compared to this relatively straightforward and secure approach, buying from a private individual involves more risk. Having said that, financially the best deals are often to be had in the private-party second-hand market. The challenge is to find them.

↑ When buying a used jet ski, don't hesitate to get the advice of a professional. He will have the diagnostic tools to evaluate the machine. This allows both buyer and seller to act with confidence.

Administrative checkpoints

THE FIRST THINGS to check are administrative matters. First, you should find out the exact year the unit was placed in service – ideally from the initial purchase invoice – and the maintenance that has been carried out since that date. An original owner with good service records is a promising start. Avoid jet skis that have been used in competitions, which is often the case for sport models, or those coming from rental businesses. If the jet ski has had several owners, check that the numbers in the owner's manual match those marked on the hull.

Technical checkpoints

EVEN WHEN BUYING from a private party, you can have the jet ski checked by a professional. This allows the seller to demonstrate the machine's true condition and the buyer to make the purchase with confidence. This practice is increasingly used for modern, complex and expensive machines. In fact, for a reasonable fee, a dealer will be able to inspect the machine, check the engine compression – which is an excellent indicator of its condition – and connect to the on-board computer if the jet ski has an electronic diagnostic system. The engine's electronics store a host of information, in particular the number of hours run – even when the computer has been disconnected – as well as engine revs and possible failures. The real demands that have been made on the machine – such as riding at sea at full throttle and tripping the rev limiter when jumping waves – can thus be assessed.

Most companies have largely perfected their diagnostic systems now – the Sea-Doo diagnostic system is exceptionally comprehensive.

Visual inspection

THE PURCHASE of a second-hand jet ski requires prior close examination to look for possible defects. The first point to check is the machine's external appearance. It is very important to see whether it has its original stickers and paint. Although the stickers affixed to the jet ski are unsightly, they are there for your safety. Check carefully that they are in place.

Checking the hull

THE FIRST THINGS to look for are the possible signs of a major repair, particularly on the front and on the sides. Collisions resulting in major damage are almost always identifiable. With double bottoms, however, it is impossible to access the hull interior for close examination. If you are in doubt, you can also check the engine compartment in the area around the driveshaft exit. In some frontal collisions, the driveshaft

↓ On this damaged machine, the driveshaft thrust bearing has been torn out, although from the exterior, the damage appears minor.

↑ When buying a used jet ski, it is important to check the hull condition by looking for small signs of weakness, especially around the front storage compartment and the engine compartment.

thrust bearing is torn off, requiring a very visible repair. Repaired hulls are rare, however. Concentrate instead on the state of the gel coat, which will always show some completely normal and unavoidable marks – if the underside of the hull is perfect, it has certainly been repainted. If this is the case you need to find out why.

Checking the jet pump

ON SOME MACHINES, the impeller condition can be checked by looking through the water intake. Get a flashlight and check the condition of the impeller, but also look for scratches on the stator – the body of the jet pump. The jet pump's water intake is often neglected when desalting. Look for traces of corrosion in this area.

Then check the condition of the ride plate under the jet pump, which should be undamaged or it could make the machine uncontrollable. Also check the water intake grate. Still in the area around the jet pump, make sure that there is no play in the steering by moving the steering nozzle while blocking the handlebar. You can also check that the mechanical or electric trim and the reverse gear are functioning properly.

On stand-up jet skis, apart from play in the steering, check for play in the area where the arm anchors to the hull and at the steering support (the mobile part that supports the handlebar).

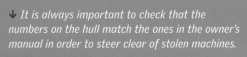

↓ It is always important to check that the numbers on the hull match the ones in the owner's manual in order to steer clear of stolen machines.

↑ On older jet skis, it is important to check the engine mounts. The engine block should always be firmly secured or it risks banging against the hull during jumps.

Checking the engine compartment

THIS IS NOT ABOUT CHECKING the internal condition of the engine, a job that at the very least requires removal of the spark plugs and taking compression readings. The condition of the engine compartment is a good indicator of the machine's overall maintenance. This compartment should be clean and well lubricated. The absence of corrosion spots is a good indication that the recommended lubrication has been carried out. Next, check the condition of certain parts to determine the exact age of the machine, in particular the engine mounts and the driveshaft's rubber coupling. On sport machines and mainly on stand-up jet skis, check carefully that the air filter and the exhaust have original parts. 'Racing' parts generally require specific adjustment, which is often neglected, thereby compromising mechanical reliability. If you are buying a machine for recreational use, beware of machines that have undergone 'pseudo soup-up' jobs. Well-tested original parts are the best guarantee of reliability for marine engines. As we saw previously in the case of a very new model, any modification can render the warranty null and void. Installation of a better ride plate to improve stability, or of an impeller, is common on older jet skis and is quite acceptable.

Checking for noise

AFTER THIS STATIC INSPECTION, the only thing left is to listen to the engine. It should run smoothly and not make any suspicious noise while idling. (Note that a two-stroke engine smokes a lot when starting cold and needs a few seconds to run correctly.) When warming up the engine, it is best to connect the flushing kit to ensure that the engine and exhaust are cooled. As well as listening for undesirable noises, check for significant engine vibration at idle, which indicates tired engine mounts. To conclude the inspection, check the condition of the floor mats, since Neoprene is rather fragile, as well as the condition of the seat, especially around the edges.

Administrative formalities

IN THE UK there is no formal legal requirement to register your jet ski centrally. Nowadays, however, there is a type of registration document that comes with new PWCs provided by a company called Datatag. While currently voluntary, the use of Datatag is growing across the UK. Each PWC is given a Datatag number which is displayed on both sides of the hull. In addition to this, datachips are placed around the inside of the PWC's engine bay that are impossible to remove. If purchasing a second-hand PWC that is registered with Datatag don't forget to inform the company about change of ownership.

Standard jet ski equipment

Driver and passenger equipment

OPERATING A JET SKI requires the correct equipment in order to maximise safety without compromising comfort or enjoyment. The various pieces of equipment used by driver and passenger are also fashion accessories, and colours tend to change with each season. However, in order to buy the right equipment we first need to understand its function and importance, and below we take a look at the shelves of a typical jet ski store.

Lifejackets

The lifejacket is the most important piece of equipment and should always be worn. From the moment you get on to a jet ski you should wear a CE-approved and preferably brightly coloured lifejacket.

Lifejacket and buoyancy aid flotation is measured in Newtons: 10 Newtons (10N) = 1kg. Always check that the lifejacket/buoyancy aid you are purchasing will support your weight. There are specialist PWC buoyancy aids which also protect against collision, but unlike lifejackets they are not guaranteed to turn you from a face-down position in the water. A proper lifejacket is essential as, in the event of loss of consciousness, the head remains above water and you can continue breathing. A lifejacket also plays the role of shock absorber in the event of a collision. You should select a model that hugs the body closely without squeezing, while allowing good freedom of movement for the arms. Some lifejackets have a small ring on the bottom for attaching the kill switch cord, a really practical detail. In addition, many of the latest models include removable back and side protections. Always choose a lifejacket that is the correct size for you (there are up to seven sizes available) and is designed especially for water sports.

The rider's equipment is important. A lifejacket should always be worn and wearing a wetsuit and helmet is strongly recommended.

The wetsuit

The wetsuit is the traditional Neoprene suit. It is not watertight, so don't expect to be completely protected in winter, even though it's true that a wetsuit keeps you quite warm. A wetsuit is close-fitting, therefore once again it is important to choose the right size. A good wetsuit is neither too heavy nor too stiff. For summer use, choose one that is between 2 and 2.5 mm thick. In addition to its thermal-protection role, the wetsuit provides some protection against blows and friction, especially when riding at sea or on a stand-up jet ski. For this reason, choose a model designed for jet ski use, which will have appropriately placed padding. There are several styles of wetsuit and they come in either one or two pieces. The two-piece models have two main advantages: they are easier to put on and you can choose not to wear the top if it is too hot. Research your wetsuit carefully to find the right one.

The shorty

This half suit affords a minimum of protection while preserving heat. As the shorty provides very little protection against impacts, it is usually reserved for summer recreation use, but remains an essential item in the jet skier's equipment.

The drysuit

With a drysuit you can brave low temperatures. A drysuit does not let water in and makes it possible for the body to stay warm, but it provides little protection in extreme conditions, the hands and feet being unprotected. While a drysuit is essential for those who want to ride in winter or in cold weather, it has its flaws. Moreover, drysuits are heavy, cumbersome, unflattering and relatively expensive to buy.

Footwear

To drive a jet ski you need comfortable footwear to give you a really good footing and thus a good driving position. The correct footwear will provide stability, support and protection. The most practical design by far is still the ankle boot designed for jet ski use. These allow you to walk on rocks, provide a firm grip even when wet and guarantee good protection, especially around the ankles. The soft sport shoes available in sports shops are inadequate, mainly because they don't provide sufficient support. Wearing this kind of shoe while riding a stand-up jet ski can be both uncomfortable and dangerous. If you don't have ankle boots, it is preferable to use a pair of sports shoes with a good, firm sole, like those meant for jogging. However, once they have been in the water, don't expect to be able to use them again for running.

Gloves

Gloves are essential in order to avoid blisters, especially during sport riding. Neoprene gloves also provide an excellent grip on the handlebar. However, they are relatively fragile and you should bear in mind that with wear and tear and the risk of misplacing them, it is not unusual to go through several pairs in a season. Always carry a replacement pair.

Goggles and masks

Riding at sea without eye protection is very uncomfortable. As well as spray, splashes and wind, there is also the sun and, even worse, the glare from the water. In short, eye protection is essential. The most effective solution is a face mask. Be sure to choose a model designed for water sports and not for all-terrain motorbikes: masks for the latter are designed to keep out dust and are closed, whereas the marine versions have openings to allow water to run out. One last important point: consider choosing a slightly tinted shield to protect you from glare. You can also go touring on a comfortable three-seater machine using simple sport sunglasses, as long as you use an eyewear retainer, like those manufactured by Croakies.

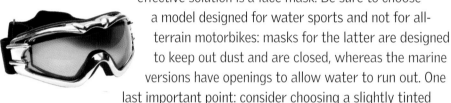

Lycra undergarments

Ideally, a jet skier's outfit should include Lycra clothing, particularly the T-shirts, with or without sleeves. Because it prevents chafing and ensures good protection against cold or sun, Lycra clothing is a must and can be bought anywhere for a few pounds. It is a good idea to have several styles – of varying thickness – among your jet ski gear.

Helmets

A helmet is essential for most water sports, especially so for sport riding at sea and above all on a stand-up jet ski. The helmet provides protection from impact against the machine in the event of a fall and has many other advantages, providing the correct rigid support for your eye protection as well as protecting the ears in the event of violent impact with the water and preventing damage to the eardrums. A helmet also provides effective protection from the sun. There are few helmets made specifically for jet skiing, but you can generally use one intended for other water sports. Choose a model with removable internal foam to facilitate cleaning, and select a simple and comfortable chin strap – you will have to choose between a system of snaps or the traditional double ring, which has the advantage of being lighter and allowing more precise tensioning. The choice is obviously a matter of personal preference. Some freestyle riders use lighter helmets to facilitate aerial tricks.

Spine guards

Spine guards are required for competitions and are also used by some recreational riders. This rigid but articulated protection for the back and spinal column offers incomparable safety for closed-course racers, where it is never advisable to fall on the track. This 'shell' is worn between the wetsuit and the lifejacket. It causes no discomfort and is light, while providing real protection.

Equipment maintenance

MAINTENANCE OF THIS equipment is often neglected, although it is every bit as important as the care lavished on the machine. The wetsuit and all accessories should be systematically rinsed with clean water. This task is all too frequently neglected or deferred. It is imperative to rinse the equipment as soon as possible after a trip, whether it was at sea or on fresh water. In both cases, the equipment will have been soiled with salt or mud and it is important to clean it quickly in order to remove this and to prevent the build-up of bad odours. You can clean your equipment with a little soap or washing-up liquid, always making sure you clean both the inside and outside of the wet gear. Again, to avoid bad odours, you must dry all equipment quickly in a well-ventilated space because it tends to retain a lot of water. Also be careful of the sun, which quickly fades the colours of Neoprene and the plastic closures. Remember the small accessories like gloves and glasses, and dry your helmet thoroughly – upside down to avoid trapping moisture. Once your equipment is quite dry, you can store it on a clothes hanger. For long garments, avoid folding the Neoprene. If a zipper is stuck, check for grains of sand or salt in the slide and clean it with a small brush. 'Greasing' zippers to keep the sand from sticking is not recommended.

To transport your gear, choose a bag that has different watertight compartments so you can store your wet gear after a trip. Don't forget to dry your bag well after the gear has been removed.

3
TECHNICAL DETAIL

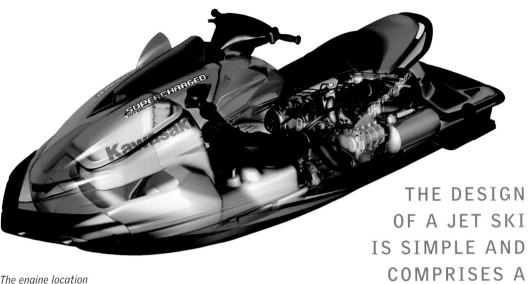

The engine location is carefully chosen to give the machine good stability.

THE DESIGN
OF A JET SKI
IS SIMPLE AND
COMPRISES A
COMPOSITE HULL,
A MULTI-CYLINDER
ENGINE (FROM TWO TO SIX
CYLINDERS) AND A JET PUMP.

The jet **pump**

TECHNICALLY SPEAKING, the jet ski's uniqueness lies in its use of a jet pump for propulsion. This feature offers many advantages, in particular the incomparable safety of a completely smooth underside, as well as very efficient performance. The jet pump provides propulsion as well as changes in direction, and stability when moving in a straight line or when turning. It is therefore the key element of a jet ski, and its characteristics determine the machine's behaviour. For this reason, it is vital to have a good understanding of how it functions in order to grasp how it affects the jet ski's response under operation. The first thing to understand is that a jet ski is not propelled by the rotation of a propeller, as on a boat, but by the water expelled from the rear of the jet pump. The latter is fed by a scoop, which is actually a water intake with a strong protective grate, located on the underside of the jet ski's hull.

Jet pump

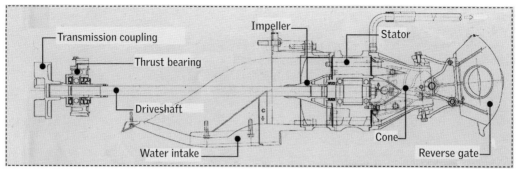

Transmission coupling · Thrust bearing · Impeller · Stator · Driveshaft · Water intake · Cone · Reverse gate

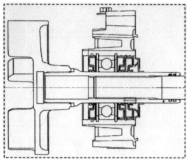

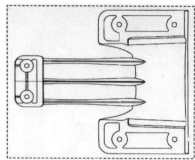

↑ While, in principle, a jet pump is very simple, its application on a jet ski is complex and determines the machine's performance.

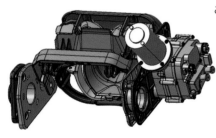

The four principal elements of a jet pump

THE JET PUMP is made up of four principal parts and, contrary to popular opinion, is not just a 'propeller in a tube'. Moreover, the term 'propeller' is theoretically incorrect in the case of a jet pump; it should be called an 'impeller'. The impeller is the pump's only moving part and is driven directly by the engine via a simple driveshaft. The impeller has a number of blades with sharp edges and rotates in a perfectly adjusted cylinder bore, the 'stator', which, as its name implies, remains static. The remainder of the jet pump consists firstly of a 'flow rectifier', also static, which improves output by stopping the flow rotation caused by the pump's impeller. The blades of the flow rectifier are tilted in the opposite direction to the impeller. And secondly, once rectified and thus brought back into a longitudinal direction, the flow is compressed in the 'fixed nozzle' to increase its speed.

Other jet pump components

A JET PUMP also has a 'cone' mounted on the outlet side of the flow rectifier and inside the fixed nozzle. This small alloy or plastic part optimises the flow and prevents cavitation, i.e. the formation of an air bubble in the moving liquid, detrimental to the pump output. Mounted on the fixed nozzle, the steering nozzle located at the jet pump's exit serves to deviate the flow to cause changes in direction. Controlled by the handlebar, the steering nozzle moves on a vertical axis. On higher-end sit-down machines with trim systems to modify the machine's plane, the steering nozzle also moves on a horizontal axis, giving it mobility on two axes. Lastly, the pump body includes a water inlet, which is used to supply the engine's cooling system, and a vacuum, which sucks out water shipped inside the hull.

The impeller and stator in detail

THE IMPELLER is technically very complex and must be paired with the stator. The number of blades on the impeller (three or four, for production machines) depends directly on the number of blades in the flow rectifier. If your impeller has an odd number of blades, you need a flow rectifier with an even number of blades, and vice versa. It is important to note that impellers have differing pitches, i.e. the blades have a complex shape with different angles. This feature enables both good start-up and high speeds on a jet ski. The impeller hub design is also very important, particularly on one with an increasing diameter, i.e. larger at the flow exit than at the entry. This special feature is really indispensable and increases the pressure and power transmitted to the water.

The shape of the flow rectifier is also very important: a small number of blades impacts directly on thrust quality, as the flow is not rectified regularly. Moreover, with fewer blades a greater angle is required to rectify the flow adequately. This greater angle acts as a barrier and thus reduces thrust. In short, with 12 blades this angle is reduced to a minimum and the initial thrust is only slowed down a little. Conversely, a large number of blades blocks the flow and reduces output. Stator design is therefore of paramount importance.

Launched in 2009, the Sea-Doo RXT was the forerunner of other high-end machines with its integration of a revolutionary suspension system offering greater riding comfort.

Trim system

NOWADAYS, with the exception of Kawasaki and some others, most production machines have a trim system. This accessory directs the jet pump flow according to navigation conditions.
The steering nozzle, which is used to change the jet ski's direction, has an additional vertical joint, which can change the direction of the jet pump's flow by a few degrees. This variation modifies the jet ski's plane and thus its behaviour in a straight line or in turns. For example, to obtain the best top speed in a straight line, you need to be on a horizontal, or better yet, a slightly elevated plane so that the machine planes easily and its draft is reduced. Conversely, on a winding course, it is preferable to have a better grip on the water with an inverse plane. The trim system reconciles these two characteristics. Trim operation is simple and is actuated from the handlebar. There are rather simple, cable-driven mechanical trim systems as well as electric ones. Each system has pros and cons. The mechanical system has the advantage of reliability and speed of action. However, the electrical system offers ease of use and is ideal for recreational applications. There are also automatic trim systems, which are used for competition riding.

The scoop and ride plate

THE JET PUMP is completed by two very important parts: the scoop, which supplies water to the pump, and the ride plate, which is located beneath the pump and is designed to keep your craft at the correct angle to the water, providing as much control and speed in as wide a variety of conditions as possible. There are many different versions of these which can easily improve the performance of production machines, particularly stand-up jet skis. While the function of the scoop is logical, the role of the plate is more complex. The latter directly influences the machine's performance by creating an efficient wake to take best advantage of the jet flow. Moreover, the plate is also responsible for a good part of the machine's 'grip' on the water. Different plates – including ones with ridges and a back extension to grip the water better – are available for all jet ski models and are significantly better than the ones you can find in mass-produced versions.

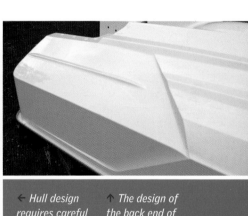

The hull

The underside of a jet ski hull, with its stiffeners, stem, intake and ride plate.

BUILT OF SYNTHETIC MATERIALS, jet ski hulls don't use any special technology, but manufacturers always look for the best material – one that is light, strong and easy to use. The hulls and decks of mass-produced models are moulded on a hot press, which facilitates fast, large-scale production. At Yamaha, the latest-generation hulls are made of NanoXcel, which saves 25kg on the final weight of the machine.

Apart from mass-produced hulls, some hulls are still handmade by skilled craftsmen, particularly those for competition and small-scale production. Freestyle and freeride jet skis, for example, have custom hulls. The latter are particularly light and are made of carbon fibre, with special designs to facilitate specific tricks.

← *Hull design requires careful consideration in order to optimise a jet ski's behaviour during operation.*

↑ *The design of the back end of a hull is essential to riding quality, as well as to optimising jet pump performance.*

Even the hull design of production machines is complex, because they must respond to such demands as holding in a turn, riding in a chop and riding at full speed. Hull design has a great impact on a jet ski's behaviour and performance, therefore the design of the stem, the bottom of the hull and the various ridges is very carefully considered.

The engine

ENGINES NOW USE state-of-the-art technology. Four-stroke multi-cylinder blocks are the most widely used and have easily overtaken the old two-stroke engines, which are now reserved for competition.

Revolution and power

THE JET SKI WORLD has recently experienced a technological revolution. Now powered by four-stroke multi-cylinder blocks, the machines have never been more sophisticated, powerful and heavy. The best example to date is the Kawasaki Ultra 260 – now the 260X – which, as its name implies, offers a respectable 260hp. Its impressive performance is obtained from a four-cylinder engine that is only 1498cm^3, thanks to a range of different technologies.

To gain an output of more than 160hp per litre, Kawasaki uses a super-charger equipped with a heat exchanger. This design features dry

↑ *The architecture of jet ski engines is comparable to that of a motorcycle, and the superchargers provide very impressive power levels.*

↑ *Yamaha offers engines with five valves per cylinder (three for the intake and two for the exhaust), after having used this technology in motorcycles.*

↑ *Sea-Doo machines have Rotax engines, which have many technical features.*

sump lubrication, fuel injection, and for distribution, two camshafts and four valves per cylinder. At the same time, the Ultra 260 has an impressive weight of 482kg ready to run!

Despite its increased complexity, the four-stroke design has been universally adopted

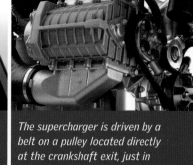

In addition to a supercharger, some engines have a heat exchanger to increase power and reliability.

The supercharger is driven by a belt on a pulley located directly at the crankshaft exit, just in front of the transmission shaft coupling.

because of its many benefits, which include lower pollution levels than two-stroke engines, quieter operation and improved reliability. Two-stroke engines – apart from those equipped with fuel injection – are reserved for competition. Derived from motorcycle engines, the four-cylinder inline architecture is the most widely used, with or without a supercharger, depending on power level. Yamaha also offers a special technology with five valves per cylinder distribution, which the company first used on its motorcycles in 1985.

Mass production of jet skis

JET SKIS ARE primarily manufactured in North America, including those made by Japanese manufacturers such as Yamaha and Kawasaki. The Atlanta-based Yamaha factory manufactures the company's jet skis for the entire world market.

Jet ski production is fairly simple. The first step is moulding the hull, its lining and deck. Each part is hot-moulded under pressure.

Cooled after coming out of the mould, each part is placed on a template for cutting and deburring.

The hulls are cut on templates.

The hull is placed on an assembly line to be fitted with its cables, engine mounts, fuel tank and jet pump.

All of the mounts, including those for the engine and the controls, are installed prior to assembly of the two parts of the hull.

The deck is placed on a second assembly line to have its equipment installed.

The fuel tank and engine are installed in the hull. In this Yamaha factory, the engine is made in Japan and arrives on the assembly line ready for installation.

A bead of glue is applied by hand to the two hull halves, which are then joined.

About 20 clamps are used to ensure a perfect hull bond.

At this point, the jet ski is nearly complete. Only its labels, rub rails and last pieces of equipment remain to be fitted.

Each machine is then put in the water for final testing, which includes checking for watertightness, as well as checking mechanical and jet pump function.

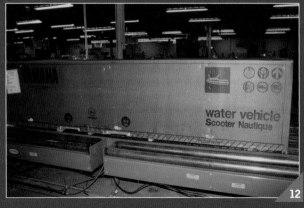

The jet ski is then packed, nearly complete, before being shipped to the dealer, who will handle set-up and delivery to the client.

Jet skis are sometimes stored before being delivered to dealers. For this reason, and for ease of transport, the packing must be as compact as possible.

4
USING A JET SKI

UK Regulations

ALTHOUGH USING A JET SKI has a number of things in common with riding a motorcycle in terms of style and technique, the formalities of owning one are certainly less stringent. In the UK, there is little in the way of national regulation governing the use of jet skis, but it is essential to be aware of and observe local rules, which vary across the country and are generally rigorously enforced. While having a licence to operate your jet ski is not a legal requirement, most authorities will want to see evidence of personal liability insurance, along with confirmation that the machine is officially recognised by checking the manufacturer's hull identification number marked on the hull itself and in your owner's manual. Most authorities will also want to check that your safety equipment is in place and appropriate, starting with your lifejacket.

Group rides require close adherence to safety rules, in particular making sure that the way is clear before changing heading and giving warning before cutting the throttle.

Licences

THE RULES OF THE WATER are not as restrictive as those of the road. Unlike with a car, there is no current legal obligation for a jet-skier to pass the equivalent of a driving test to demonstrate their competence. Emphasis is on education rather than legislation and you are encouraged to learn your jet-skiing skills through courses provided by the RYA and affiliated centres.

Jet-skiing around the coast of the UK or further out to sea is open to all and does not require a licence, but attention must be paid to local regulations, particularly the speed limit. Ignorance of local by-laws and restrictions is no excuse and you must expect to be held fully responsible for your actions and possibly fined by the local authority if you transgress.

Use of inland waterways is also highly regulated and you should contact the appropriate local authority in order to discover its regulations and, where applicable, to register your jet ski. Registration is compulsory on many inland waterways, and increasingly authorities also insist that you hold an International Certificate of Competence (ICC). This is a certificate that is recognised internationally and provides documentary evidence that the holder has attended a formally recognised training course and reached the required level of competence through an assessment of their skills. It is, in effect, a licence to use the waterways in question but is not in itself a qualification. The ICC certificate is required for almost all inland waterways in Europe as well as the coastal waters of the Mediterranean. However, it is not compulsory in many of the coastal areas of northern Europe and the advice, once again, is to plan ahead and check with the local authority of the area you are planning to visit.

The Personal Watercraft Competency course offered by the RYA will provide you with a good working knowledge of passage planning, decision making, and launching,

Jet ski use in the UK

For the driver	For the machine
• Boat licence	• Hull identification number
• Lifejacket	• Insurance
	• Clearly visible registration number
	• Safety equipment: a hand flare, and a rope equal to at least three times the machine's length

While a licence is not a national requirement in the UK many authorities will ask for evidence of competency in the form of an ICC.

handling and recovery skills. Children between the age of 12 and 16 who take the course will have their certificates endorsed to show that they may only use a jet ski under the supervision of a responsible adult.

The ICC certificate is available to all UK nationals over the age of 16. In order to apply you will need to provide evidence of both residence and of competence with your machine. The usual way to do this is to provide an RYA certificate indicating that you have satisfactorily completed a relevant practical course at a recognised RYA training centre or at a club affiliated to the RYA that is authorised to carry out tests.

Teaching the RYA PWC Competency course

IF YOU ARE INTERESTED in sharing your knowledge and skills with others, the RYA offers a course to enable you to teach the essentials of jet-skiing. To be eligible for this course you must hold: an RYA PWC

certificate of competence and an RYA first-aid certificate, and have had five years' part-time or one season full-time jet ski handling experience.

Riding a jet ski at night is forbidden in many countries. Keep this in mind when organising excursions at sea.

Rules and Restrictions

AS THERE IS NO NATIONAL 'rule book' for the use of jet skis, the regulations and restrictions that jet-skiers must abide by depend on the waters to be used and you must contact the local authority concerned to discover exactly what those rules are. The dependence on local rules makes sense in the case of inland waterways since the nature and size of each can vary enormously.

When jet-skiing offshore, most authorities will set a zone from the shore within which jet-skiers must keep to a very low speed limit to avoid interfering with or causing danger to other close-to-shore activities. Typically this may be 200 or 300 metres with a maximum speed of 5 to 8 knots. There are also usually restrictions in terms of noise limits, and jet-skiing at night is forbidden almost everywhere – indeed, very few jet skis have any form of headlamp.

While jet ski registration is not mandatory everywhere, many local authorities will require you to register with them before allowing you to use their waterways.

The key restrictions to using inland waterways are again likely to cover speed and noise limits as well as an insistence on carrying appropriate safety equipment, including a lifejacket/buoyancy aid and a kill cord.

It cannot be emphasised too strongly that local rules and restrictions must be adhered to and that ignorance will not be accepted as a defence in any breach of the local by-laws. Jet-skiing is closely monitored, especially during the summer, and breaches of the regulations can be severely punished. If using your jet ski abroad, you should be aware that breaches are often dealt with particularly severely. In France, for example, speeding inside the 300 metre exclusion zone is punishable by a fine of up to 3,750 euros and/or six months' imprisonment, while misuse of distress flares carries a penalty of a fine up to 30,000 euros and/or two years' imprisonment.

The most important rule to observe is the speed limit.

The labels affixed to the jet ski are there for your safety.

Insurance

PROPER INSURANCE cover for both your jet ski and trailer, as well as personal liability, is extremely important and you need it to be able to register your jet ski with many local authorities. Common sense will tell you that wherever you plan to jet-ski, good insurance cover is essential: the risk of accident cannot be ignored. Some agents specialise in covering these risks, but you should compare their rates carefully because there are great disparities between the various companies. Many companies offer cheaper insurance if you have an ICC certificate. The cost of insurance for a jet ski is modest considering the high price of modern machines.

Where to launch?

IN BRIEF, before launching make sure that local regulations permit jet ski operation. To find launching sites, contact the local authorities, such as the harbour office or the city council. It is sometimes difficult to obtain reliable information quickly. You can also contact the local jet ski dealer, who will know the local rules well. Moreover, he can inform you of any risks or dangers in the area. You can also use the Internet to find out about accessible launching places, especially through sites and forums such as www.jetski.com and www.boatlaunch.co.uk.

On-board essentials

OPERATING A JET SKI imposes certain obligations. You must **always** be able to show your papers to public safety officials, including your ICC certificate if required, local registration document and proof of ownership along with the hull identification number. It is advisable to keep your documentation in a small, watertight plastic bag. In addition to your papers, you must be able to demonstrate that the required safety equipment is on board and in good order.

In the interest of safety, you are also recommended to carry the following:

- full tank of fuel
- small fire extinguisher
- flare pack (orange smoke flares and red hand-held flares)
- knife
- torch
- tool kit
- first-aid kit
- folding paddle
- small folding anchor
- 5 metre length of 8mm towline

Additionally, for offshore riding you should carry a compass, charts and VHF or mobile phone, and you are strongly recommended to make a passage plan and inform someone of your route and the ETA for both your destination and return.

↑ *Each machine has a compartment for a fire extinguisher, which is highly recommended in the UK.*

← *It is essential when cruising offshore to carry a flare pack and a towline.*

Rescue at sea

IN THE CASE OF AN EMERGENCY you need to be aware of the options open to you. Always stay with your jet ski – it will be far easier for your rescuers to spot you with your machine.

▶ **If people are in sight** *use the international distress signal – slowly raise and lower your arms in two wide arcs.*

▶ **If you have a VHF radio** *with you, call the Coastguard on channel 16. If using a mobile, call 999 and ask for the Coastguard.*

▶ **When firing flares,** *ensure that you let them off downwind to avoid the risk of burning yourself or setting the jet ski alight.*

Transport and maintenance

↓ *Although often used in the US, a pickup truck is not an ideal solution for a variety of reasons, including its high loading bed.*

USE OF A JET SKI requires transportation and it is vital to have a practical, functional and safe system. The trailer is an essential item for transportation, launching and storage. For recreational jet skiing, the trailer also offers an efficient and practical platform for maintenance tasks. The trailer is therefore essential to the use of a jet ski because of its many practical applications.

Trailer types

ALL JET SKI TRAILERS are built on pretty much the same design: a frame on a single axle (easier to manoeuvre), with dismountable or retractable rear lights to allow the frame to go in the water, and a winch for loading and unloading the machine. There are also models for transporting one, two or three jet skis as well as other options. To choose the right trailer, it is important to identify the conditions under which it will be used. If, for example, the jet ski will be used just a few miles from home and the trailer will be used primarily for launching, you should choose a light, compact model with easy-to-remove lights and an easy loading system for the jet ski. Conversely, if you plan to tow the jet ski over long distances, it would be better to opt for a trailer equipped with large wheels (12 to 13 inches/30 to 33 cm) so it can be towed on the motorway without difficulty. Bear in mind that while a 'heavy' trailer is perfect for the road, it will be cumbersome for launching.

The final consideration is the towing vehicle. If you have a vehicle with torque and good traction, like a 4x4, launching and retrieving the jet ski on rough ground or a slippery ramp will be easy. But if you have a lighter vehicle, especially one with front-wheel drive, you would be well advised to choose a light and compact trailer to avoid discovering that you can't get your machine out of the water because of its weight. There are also tyres made specially for sand. With a broader balloon shape and lower air pressure, they make it possible to reach the water's edge, especially on the coast, but their road use is more restricted.

← The 4x4 is the best vehicle for towing a jet ski. It also facilitates launching and retrieval.

↑ Quad bikes are often used for launching by professionals and sportsmen. The quad bike enables you to reach areas with difficult access.

How to tie down a jet ski

MOST TRAILERS have efficient and practical tie-down systems, usually with a bow guard in the front to prevent longitudinal movement and side pads for lateral support. A perfectly designed trailer with well-adjusted fittings only needs a simple strap to secure the back of the jet ski to the trailer. You should never fasten the jet ski at the handlebar or the seat. For adjustable trailers designed to take any type of machine, it is advisable to check that the entire unit is well balanced.

To tie a machine down properly, a strap in the front, as well as one or two at the rear, is a must.

Count on 30 to 50 kg on the tongue, ie the mass on the ball of the towing vehicle. Balanced in this way, a loaded trailer will have less of a tendency to sway. When transporting a stand-up jet ski, the machine's arm must be strapped with a bungee cord to prevent it from swinging. Like boat trailers, jet ski trailers used to have rubber rollers for sliding the machine on, but modern jet ski trailers are now fitted with pads, which have the advantage of offering a larger contact surface rather than three or four support points. This considerably reduces the risk of hull damage during transportation. When wet, the pads also facilitate retrieving the machine from the water and guide it more effectively.

Launching

LAUNCHING IS SIMPLE, but some precautions should be taken. While in some cases a jet ski can be launched by one person, it is more easily done by two (one at the wheel of the car and the other to deal with the jet ski). Before launching, it is essential to start the jet ski's engine for a few seconds to be sure that it works properly, and to be sure that the kill switch key is with the machine. Also check that the drain plugs are tightly closed and locked. After checking these items, it is a good idea to inspect the launching area, especially if the ramp is not concreted or if you are using it for the first time. While in theory it is advisable to avoid getting the trailer wheels completely in the water – especially in salt water – to preserve the bearings, in practice waves make it difficult to follow this recommendation. For this reason, many jet skiers prefer to immerse their trailer for ease of handling and then carefully maintain it by checking the condition of the bearings after each launch and replacing them every year.

It is better to have two people when launching, one person to stay at the wheel of the car and the other to launch the machine.

← This trailer, designed specifically for jet skis, has raised mobile rear lights, which facilitates launching.

→ Equipped with wide tyres, this launching trailer is meant for use on sand; it is not allowed on the road.

Driving with a trailer

AS A STAND-UP jet ski on a small single-unit trailer weighs less than 200kg, it can easily be towed by any vehicle. Attention just needs to be paid to the trailer's overhang in tight turns. When reversing (the beginner's dread), you must remember to focus on the trailer's position first, then that of the towing vehicle. The hard part is reversing your normal manoeuvres: for example, to direct the trailer towards the left, you have to steer the back of the car towards the right. Reversing with a trailer requires that you go slowly and make constant steering adjustments. In the event of a problem, moving forward a little is often helpful. On the road, if the trailer is not wider than the towing vehicle there are no particular problems, going over speed bumps at walking speed being the principal constraint. Driving on motorways is also very simple and does not require particular vigilance. Having said that, if the trailer has small wheels (12 inches/30cm or less), it is best to reduce your cruising speed to prevent its tyres and bearings from heating up.

Guidance for towing a jet ski trailer

BEFORE TOWING a trailer you should ensure that the classification of your driving licence will allow you to do so. Licences obtained after January 1997 may require an additional endorsement and new drivers are restricted to the following combinations: Vehicles up to 3.5 tonnes (Cat B) with a 750kg trailer (4.25 tonnes total mass weight); and Category B vehicles with larger trailers (over 750kg), provided that the combined weight does not exceed 3.5 tonnes and the gross weight of the trailer does not exceed the unladen weight of the towing vehicle. The trailer must have a registration plate identical to the plate on the towing vehicle. In all cases, the maximum permitted speed when towing a trailer on the motorway is 60mph, and on a dual carriageway it is 50mph.

Avoiding front-wheel spin The launching ramp is wet and very slippery and this can lead to you not having enough traction to tow your jet ski and trailer out of the water with a front-wheel-drive vehicle. To solve this problem, you should try to set the trailer's jockey wheel so that it supports most of the trailer's weight, which will allow the towing vehicle to regain traction.

Trailer maintenance

THE WHEELS and the electrical parts should be the focus of trailer maintenance. For the wheels, checking the condition of the bearings is a must prior to each departure. You should check for play in the wheels. Note also that a defective bearing is easily identified by a growling noise while driving; you should replace the defective part at the slightest sign of this or you risk having a wheel seize from overheating and a tyre blowout when travelling under load.

To check the condition of the wheel bearings, you have to raise the trailer with a jack and turn the wheel by hand. There shouldn't be any hard spots.

The tyres should also be inspected for wear and signs of damage, and the tyre pressure should be regularly checked. Electrical maintenance should focus on the rear lights, which are prone to severe oxidation. If a bulb doesn't work, the connection may need cleaning. When reassembling it, you may like to consider putting a little marine grease on the thimbles and screws to inhibit corrosion.

← The tyre tread wear limit is 1.6mm. Tyres in good condition reduce the risk of a puncture.

← When carrying out trailer maintenance, it is important to grease the hitch as well as the jockey wheel, as both are very exposed to corrosion.

↑ A trailer hoist with a strap or a rope is easier to use than one with a metal cable. It is important to grease the non-return ratchet as part of your maintenance.

Launching carts

SOMETIMES, access to the water is not suitable for a motor vehicle, particularly in the case of beaches at low tide. In this situation, a launching cart is quite useful. Take care, however, because this accessory is reserved for stand-up jet skis and it takes a lot of work to get the machine out of the water – three or even four people are not too many – so you shouldn't think of a cart as a universal solution, even if it is a very useful piece of equipment for many situations, particularly when moving a jet ski without a trailer.

No trailer?

IS IT POSSIBLE to transport a jet ski without a trailer? Really, the only viable alternative is a small van. A van has the advantage of being more manoeuvrable than a trailer and keeps the machine and equipment safe from inquisitive eyes. For this reason, it is favoured by frequent riders and competitors. Pickup trucks generally have very high beds and are short, making it impossible to close the back gate. Moreover, securing the machine is never very easy without a specific cradle. A big estate car could possibly transport a stand-up jet ski, but remember that a jet ski remains wet for a long time after use due to water draining from the exhaust and cooling system, so you are likely to fill the car with dirty water.

For stand-up jet skis, a launching cart is not only handy for reaching some spots but also makes it easier to store the machine and perform maintenance tasks.

5
JET SKI OPERATION

OPERATING A JET SKI is very simple in the case of sit-down machines, but stand-up models require more technical ability. We look closely at the comparative design details later in this book. There are some things that all machines have in common, however, and these are dictated by the jet ski design itself, especially its jet propulsion.

EACH MACHINE HAS ITS OWN WAY OF BEHAVING AND HOLDING IN A TURN, AND EACH IS DIFFERENT IN TERMS OF ITS EFFICIENCY AND THE THRILLS IT PROVIDES.

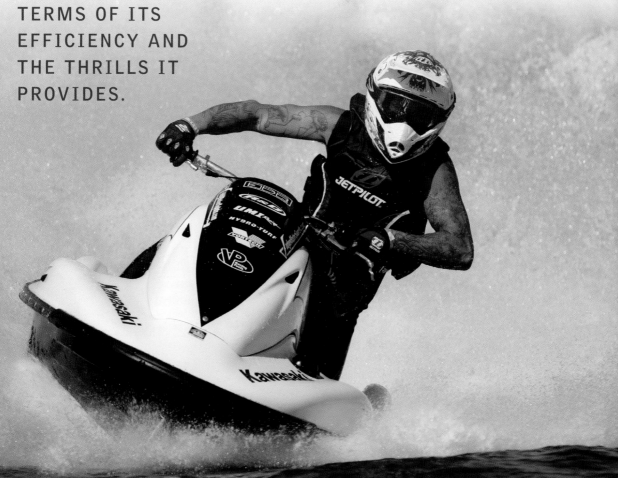

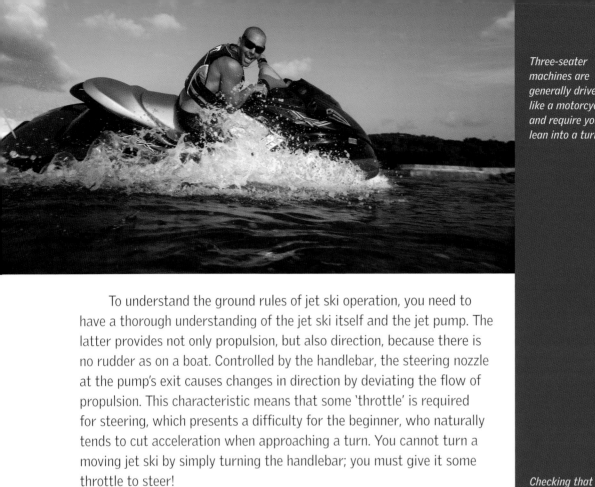

Three-seater machines are generally driven like a motorcycle and require you to lean into a turn.

To understand the ground rules of jet ski operation, you need to have a thorough understanding of the jet ski itself and the jet pump. The latter provides not only propulsion, but also direction, because there is no rudder as on a boat. Controlled by the handlebar, the steering nozzle at the pump's exit causes changes in direction by deviating the flow of propulsion. This characteristic means that some 'throttle' is required for steering, which presents a difficulty for the beginner, who naturally tends to cut acceleration when approaching a turn. You cannot turn a moving jet ski by simply turning the handlebar; you must give it some throttle to steer!

Checking that the way is clear before turning should become an automatic reflex.

The second ground rule for jet ski operation is to understand that there is no means of deceleration, except for on certain high-end models. Without brakes, a jet ski's momentum can carry it for several tens of metres. This requires some training to master, particularly for docking. It is clear, then, that perfect control of the accelerator is a key requirement for jet ski operation, whether for running, turning or simply stopping. This point is even more important on a stand-up jet ski, because the jet flow impacts directly on the machine's stability. To really appreciate this aspect of a jet ski, you need to understand its technical characteristics and how to handle the accelerator.

Master the accelerator

BEFORE RIDING for the first time, it is imperative to have perfect control of the throttle lever and especially to know how to use it gradually and proportionally. You have to keep in mind that the throttle lever is not an 'on/off' button. Cutting the throttle should become a natural reflex. This 'dry run' training will help you avoid tensing up on the accelerator when you first start riding. A jet ski usually gives a beginner a sense of power, so it is important to understand and anticipate this feeling.

While a jet ski is easy to operate, it has no brakes, so it is important to understand how to use the accelerator.

Know before you go

BEFORE GOING RIDING, especially at sea, it is a good idea to go through a mini checklist, not only to ensure your safety, but also quite simply to avoid spoiling a good time. When launching, you should always make sure that the engine will dry-start to avoid finding yourself on the water with a broken-down machine. By doing this, you will also ensure that you have the indispensable kill switch key with you. Then you should make sure that the jet ski is ready for operation, starting with checking the fuel level and that the fuel valve is correctly positioned to 'on' – a wise precaution that will prevent you running out of fuel in the middle of the water. Before leaving, you should also check that the storage compartment, engine compartment and drain plugs are closed to prevent water getting in, and make sure that the seals are well positioned and not pinched.

A great means of discovery, the jet ski allows you to land easily. Just be careful to avoid water that is too shallow (less than 60cm).

Beginner's checklist

BEFORE RIDING a sit-down or stand-up machine, the beginner must understand some essential points – first and foremost, that you should board a jet ski from the back and not from the side. Before boarding, it is advisable to take a few minutes while in shallow water to locate the grab handles and the boarding step, if the jet ski has one. You should also locate and test the operation of the kill switch so there is no possibility of finding yourself at sea without knowing how to shut off the machine in an emergency. The same goes for the controls on the handlebar, in particular the start button and the emergency stop. Lastly, it is imperative to know how the fuel valve operates. You must familiarise yourself with these things before operating a jet ski.

Boarding a jet ski must be done from the rear of the machine.

Safety always

WHATEVER ITS DESIGN, a jet ski is fairly easy to use and has only a few safety requirements; jet ski use is still quite relaxed and hassle-free. To ensure your safety, all you need to do is observe some obvious and sensible rules. First of all, the kill switch: attach it correctly, either to your wrist or directly to your lifejacket. Both choices have their advantages; it is simply a matter of personal preference. Do not under any circumstances leave it on the handlebar, because in the event of a fall, you will be unable to catch up with a runaway machine, especially in rough seas.

Operating a jet ski can be quite simple and is within the reach of all experience levels.

A lifejacket not only makes it possible to stay afloat but also keeps the head out of water in the event of loss of consciousness. It also absorbs part of the shock in the event of violent impact with the water or even with the machine. It just doesn't make any sense not to wear one. Remember that in the event of a collision or a fall, one of the risks associated with using a jet ski is being knocked unconscious. The lifejacket is your most important item of safety equipment. Apart from these safety considerations, you must also be aware of the weather forecast and the times of the tides before going to sea, even if you are only going a few hundred metres off the coast.

Some technical information

THE BEGINNER needs to understand how certain pieces of equipment on a jet ski work in order to be able to operate them. The engine's cooling system has a small water outlet on the deck of the machine. This tiny hole, which is located forward and in full view, allows you to check that water is circulating correctly in the cooling system. If, with the engine running, water does not run out or only a little runs out, the system is blocked, cooling is not taking place and there is a major risk of the engine overheating and being irreparably damaged. Should a problem occur, turn the engine off immediately and check the system.

Next, all jet skis have a bilge pump for removing the water that gets inside the hull. This pump is driven by the vacuum from the jet pump, therefore it needs a certain engine speed to function: idling does not provide the needed suction. For this reason, installing an additional electric bilge pump is highly recommended for stand-up jet skis. If, while riding, you notice that your jet ski has shipped water – a phenomenon identifiable by an awareness of weight and hull imbalance – you should ride a little in a straight line at medium speed so that the automatic bilge pump empties the hull. Try to get closer to a docking point, in case the ingress of water is due to real damage and not to the normal functioning of the machine. With a little experience, you will get to know your machine perfectly and will quickly be able to distinguish between a normal intrusion of water and a real problem. Some machines also have a vertical water jet placed at the back of the jet pump. This jet, which can reach more than 3 metres high, is used to locate the machine in the middle of the waves and is therefore a useful safety item for navigation at sea.

Modern jet skis now have a 'key' to limit the engine power for safe learning.

Learning key

USING THE THROTTLE control correctly is one of the first things you should learn. To help with this, some manufacturers have adopted an electronic learning system. Called the 'Learning Key' by Sea-Doo, these systems electronically limit engine output according to the safety key plugged into the machine – there are two colour-coded keys. These very effective systems allow the whole family to use the same machine, even a very powerful one. This device, which is often installed on modern machines, is rarely found on older models or stand-up jet skis.

Clean your jet pump

AFTER LANDING on a beach or at the edge of a lake, the pump generally sucks in pebbles or sand brought in by the waves; when starting up the engine, this material is likely to pass through the jet pump and serious damage could result. There is an easy way to clean your jet pump and therefore avoid damaging it: bring your machine into 60 or 70 cm of water and rock the rear up and down five or six times to make the water go in and out, which will drain the pump. Obviously, this operation is easier with a light jet ski, but it can really help save the jet pump.

Also, if, while riding, your jet pump begins to cavitate, ie the pump output is not as good, it is probable that the supply to the pump has been disrupted by a foreign object. Something as simple as a little piece of plastic bag, algae or rope wedged in the intake grate can have very serious consequences. (You can also easily detect this problem on machines equipped with a rev counter by checking the speed of the engine compared to your speed over the water.) If you notice any cavitation, you can simply cut the engine and, with the suction stopped, the foreign body should then fall off. If the problem persists in spite of this operation, then the clogging items need to be removed by hand. To do this, you can either go to the shore's edge and lay the machine on its side (while still in the water), or, if you are on open water, you can do it by feel, by passing your hand over the water intake. In both cases, it is imperative to remove the kill switch key to prevent any unexpected movement and, in particular, the engine starting. This problem is quite common and in 90 per cent of cases this small intervention will be effective. If not, the only thing left is to dismantle the pump.

Operating a sit-down jet ski

THERE ARE NO PARTICULAR problems associated with operating a sit-down jet ski (also known as a 'runabout'), at least not on calm water and on a machine that is not too powerful. At sea, with over 250hp under the throttle, you obviously need to have a certain level of technical skill and be in good physical condition; beginners can often underestimate the importance of this last point. Apart from that, riding a jet ski depends primarily on the machine and its destination.

There are two types of sit-down jet ski: some machines need the rider to lean to change direction, while others require you to remain as upright as possible to be able to turn. In the first case, the sensation is not unlike the feeling provided by a motorcycle, as the rider is firstly forced to move towards the inside of the turn, and then to find the right position to ensure the best re-acceleration when increasing the throttle, which is moving backwards to guarantee the best plane for the machine. The second type requires the rider to move towards the outside, as when riding a quad bike. This movement is both very efficient and very physical, and many view it as the more exhilarating of the two. Each machine requires a particular style of riding and operation, using the angle and position of the rider's body to modify the machine's plane when accelerating, going in or out of a turn, riding in a chop and going over waves.

Getting started on a sit-down jet ski

RIDING A SIT-DOWN jet ski is a simple activity, which puts the design within reach of all experience levels. If you have never ridden a jet ski, rest assured that learning is easy and fast. In less than 20 minutes you should have established the basic techniques required. The advantage of this design for the beginner is ease of handling. To get started, you have to put the machine in at least 70cm of water and board from the rear, taking care, if it is a small machine, not to destabilise the jet ski. Then you should connect your kill switch key and move off without accelerating. All you have to do now is accelerate very gradually to move away from the shore. Be sure to observe the local speed-limit and safety-zone regulations.

Riding in groups on an excursion requires constant vigilance to avoid collisions. Always check that the way is clear before changing course.

On the water, first you will have to learn and understand the operation of the throttle lever and the handlebar, and especially the interaction between these two controls. Your first exercises will therefore consist of riding in some straight lines at low speed in a clear zone and trying to stop. This little exercise will convince you of the amount of distance needed to 'stop' a jet ski's momentum. Then you will have to try turning. The fastest way to learn to do this is by simply going in circles in the water and by progressively widening the radius of your circle. Take care to reverse the direction and to test various positions for your body and angles for the machine. This exercise can appear simplistic, but you will quickly learn about the functioning and behaviour of a jet ski. Moreover, it forces the rider to accelerate and turn simultaneously. Being able to do these two things at the same time is the basis for controlling a jet ski. Once you master them, you can ride a jet ski. However, you still have to learn how to be in full control ...

Avoid collisions

LOOK BEFORE TURNING. Warn before stopping. On the water, whether you are riding at sea or on an inland waterway, one of the principal dangers is collision with another jet ski. It is therefore important to avoid crowds, especially when learning. From the start, develop the habit of systematically glancing around before changing course. Some machines have rear-view mirrors, but don't trust them – it is always safer to look around. In the same vein, if you ride in a group, always give warning before cutting the throttle by raising your left arm and making sure that no one is in your wake.

Precautions for towables

'TOWABLES' includes all of the equipment that can be towed by a jet ski. They can provide thrills of their own, because they benefit from the machine's acceleration and its ability to turn sharply, as well as from the safety offered by the jet pump.

Having said that, 'playing' with towables imposes certain requirements on the jet ski operator. In a turn, with only a dozen metres of rope between it and the machine, a towable does not follow the same trajectory as the jet ski. Pulled by the centrifugal force and retained by the length of the line, its turn is much wider. The towable cannot modify its trajectory or speed and is therefore completely at the mercy of the towing jet ski. The machine's rider must constantly be aware of this and be particularly careful not to turn or swing near the shore or beach, to avoid forcing the float onto dry land, which is the most common cause of accidents. You also need room to swing and must be sure that no one else is swinging close to you, as it is virtually impossible for a towable to take

You must also watch your speed. A float does not have the navigation capacities of a jet ski. It jumps a lot and, at speed, the water surface is hard. Special care is required, especially at sea. Some basic equipment is also essential: ideally a wet/drysuit, a lifejacket, glasses and gloves. It is also a good idea to place a pennant in the middle of the rope. As with waterskiing, a passenger must keep a constant watch on the towable.

↓ Only three-seater jet skis should be used for towing, as it is important to have a co-pilot and the ability to reboard the person being towed.

Operating a stand-up jet ski is by far the most physically demanding, but it also offers the greatest thrills on fresh water.

Getting started on a stand-up jet ski

RIDING A STAND-UP jet ski has the reputation of being very difficult – both physically trying and discouraging for beginners. This bad press is not completely unfounded, but it results primarily from lack of training. The error lies in trying to ride a stand-up jet ski without knowing the ground rules. The beginner gets worn out by the constant reboarding and eventually gets discouraged. With a little instruction, anyone in good physical condition can learn to ride a stand-up jet ski in less than half a day.

First of all, you have to be well equipped. A full wetsuit keeps you from hurting your legs and from getting cold. Obviously, the learning environment is also very important. It is so much easier to begin learning in calm, warm water than in choppy, freezing water. Without instruction, it is not worth trying to learn in cold water; that is the best way to become physically exhausted and discouraged. The learning space is also important. It has to be clear and free of rocks and other hazards, and well away from other users, especially swimmers. To facilitate boarding and taking off, the learner should start out at the right depth, say between 70 and 100 cm of water, so that he or she can stand on the bottom.

The position of the handle pole has no impact on the control of the machine, but rather allows it to follow the rider's movements to take advantage of the best riding position.

The position of the feet and legs is very important, particularly placing a foot at the rear of the deck.

Don't choose a place that is too shallow, otherwise you risk sucking sand or pebbles into the jet pump and damaging the impeller. When riding in lakes, watch out for mud, which makes your shoes stick to the bottom and the back deck very slippery.

Boarding

FIRST, YOU SHOULD get someone to help you by holding the jet ski steady when you are stationary and for the first metre of take-off, just like at the start of a race. This helps you find your balance more quickly. Before taking off, you have to connect the kill switch key and position yourself behind the machine. With one leg standing on the bottom, bend your other leg and place the knee on the machine's deck. With both hands on the handlebar, all that's left to do now is to start the engine without accelerating.

Kneel before you stand

AS PREVIOUSLY mentioned, the accelerator is the most important control on a jet ski. This is even more true for a stand-up model, because the jet flow also stabilises the machine. Jet flow is key to stability as well as change of direction. Having perfect throttle control is even more of a requirement for a stand-up jet ski than for a sit-down model; you need a few 'revs' to ride and turn. You must also avoid any jolts to prevent destabilising the jet ski. To get started successfully, you should kneel and not try to stand up immediately. Once starting and taking off have been mastered, the beginner should focus on learning how the machine behaves from a kneeling position, as this makes the jet ski much easier to manoeuvre. You must have perfect control of the accelerator and be able to turn right, left and go in a straight line before trying to stand up. Kneeling enables you to learn more quickly how to balance and to have fun instead of getting worn out by falling off over and over again.

Once you have mastered balancing and operating the jet ski from a kneeling position, you can gradually try to stand up. Ride at medium speed in a straight line and try to stand up for a few metres. It is better to go slowly and return to a kneeling position if you have trouble, or when approaching a turn, to avoid the falls that are so tiring to the beginner. So, stand up gradually – at first for just a few metres, then for a few hundred metres. Once you can travel in a straight line with perfect control, try

Riding a stand-up jet ski requires a lot of technique to master leaning and positioning your body, as well as controlling the accelerator and the handlebar position.

changing course. Then try increasingly tight turns. It is often easier for beginners to turn in one direction than the other. If it is easier for you to turn to the left, don't hesitate to follow a circuit that turns to the left so you can progress more quickly. However, once you can turn successfully in one direction, use your experience to help you learn how to turn the other way.

Improving your performance on a stand-up jet ski

RIDING A STAND-UP jet ski requires good technique as well as being in good physical condition. It takes a lot of practice to improve. If thrills are your goal, the art of riding lies first and foremost in finding the correct position to get the best weight distribution and ideal centre of gravity. As when riding a motorcycle on a circuit, the jet skier will therefore try to lower his centre of gravity or move it towards the inside of a turn, while taking care to keep enough weight on the jet ski's deck not to come 'unstuck'.

Spin-out, the first 'trick'

WHILE THE FIRST STEPS of learning to ride a stand-up jet ski may not be much fun, developing your riding technique is exciting. By following the advice above, you can start to master your machine and understand its behaviour with less than a day's practice. Part of this is having your first involuntary 'spin-out'. While this usually ends with the novice stand-up jet ski rider in the water, you can learn a lot from it.

A spin-out is when the back of the jet ski skids and slides over the water. As the jet pump is not being properly fed with water, the accelerator stops working. This 'trick' is generally the result of not taking a turn correctly or of too violent a swerve. You really have to learn how to prevent it for yourself through trial and error.

Reboarding in deep water

REBOARDING IN DEEP water is harder on a stand-up jet ski because it is impossible to push off the bottom to climb onto it. This means that more effort and preparation are required. First, you must stabilise the machine and then you have to act quickly. Because of the precarious balancing when boarding, you should always reconnect the kill switch before reboarding and take off quickly to gain stability with a minimum of throttle.

Reboarding is greatly facilitated by a boarding step. Without it, particularly on a stand-up jet ski, major physical effort is required.

In the event of a capsize

CAPSIZING IS MORE common on a stand-up jet ski than on sit-down models, but the procedure to follow to get the machine floating again is identical in both cases. You need to understand two important things: firstly, that there is generally a correct righting direction; and secondly, that you should position yourself at the rear of the machine and not on the side. Obviously, it is preferable to do everything as quickly as possible in order to prevent the intrusion of water and to avoid sucking air into the fuel system. The righting direction is often determined by the location of the engine compartment air intake in order to limit the entry of water into the hull. The correct righting direction is clearly indicated on a sticker at the back of the machine. At sea, surrounded by waves, the operation can be difficult and requires a perfect grip on the machine. It is especially important to hold the outermost edge of the deck to gain the best leverage. In a large swell, you must be careful to choose the right moment for righting, ie after the wave has passed and always perpendicular to it. Righting is directly associated with restarting.

Once the machine is upright, prepare your kill switch key, reboard and quickly restart the engine. As water intrusion is inevitable after a capsize, ride in a straight line a few times at medium speed to empty the hull. If your machine has a bilge pump, activate it quickly. Righting and reboarding a jet ski at sea is a tiring operation; you should always allow yourself a recovery period to avoid getting sore muscles.

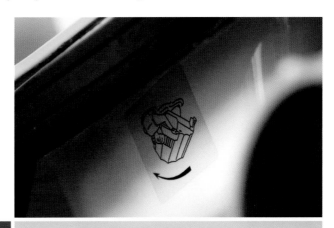

In case of a capsize, some machines have a precise righting direction in order to avoid shipping water into the hull. This is clearly indicated on a sticker placed at the rear of the hull.

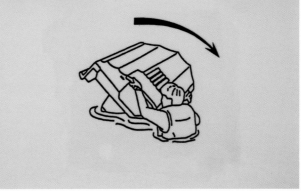

Leg-in-the-water technique

BOTH SPECTACULAR and effective, the leg-in-the-water technique, when used on a stand-up jet ski, allows you to turn at high speed. This technique has its supporters and its opponents and can be used for both wide and tight turns. In both cases, this technique works best in calm water and requires you to be in good physical condition. When going through fast turns, it is sometimes useful to put the inside foot in the water to provide a 'pivot point' that facilitates slight changes in course.

For tighter turns, the technique is a little different, because the aim is to move the centre of gravity lower and as much towards the inside as possible in order to turn quickly – even making the turn into a hairpin. In this case, not only the instep, but also the leg and even the knee can make contact with the water surface and slide over it. The best way to learn this technique is to be on a closed course so you have constant points of reference. The leg that remains on the machine must be well positioned. For example, in the case of a turn to the left, the right leg is of course standing on the right side of the deck; the foot on the inside of the turn (the left) is outside the hull and enters the water gradually as you go into the turn. At the same time, it is important to bend the legs and to place the foot a bit aft to make it easier to lower your torso. Once the turning point is crossed, all you have to do is accelerate to straighten the machine.

Putting a leg in the water allows you to turn efficiently.

To move from theory to practice, be ready for some impressive 'tricks'; then it is up to you to find the right way to use this technique to best effect.

Jet ski courses

THE ROYAL YACHTING ASSOCIATION (RYA) organises courses covering different levels of competency. Increasingly their PW certificate is required by local harbour authorities and is also likely to be needed if you want to use your PWC abroad (check with the authorities of the area you are visiting).

6

MAINTENANCE

Routine maintenance

CONTRARY TO POPULAR OPINION, jet ski maintenance is within the capability of most people, both in terms of level of difficulty and expense. This is due mainly to the small number of wearing parts. Routine maintenance consists of simple tasks performed on the engine and the jet pump. However, if these basic tasks are neglected, the consequences can be severe. Jet ski maintenance is primarily aimed at protecting it from condensation and the potentially harmful elements in which it is used: fresh water, salt water and sand.

The tools needed to repair your jet ski are brand-specific and are only available from the manufacturer. They can be difficult for end-users to obtain.

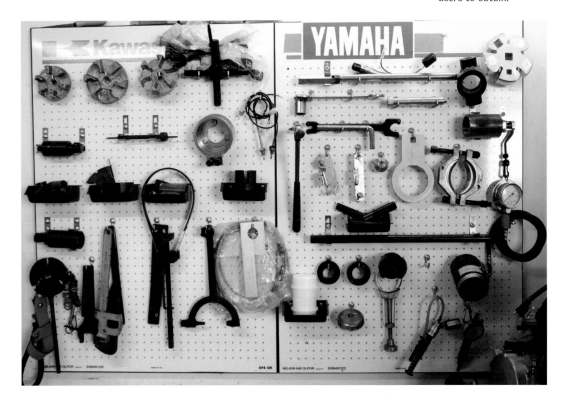

Desalting

IT IS IMPERATIVE TO DESALT your jet ski after every open water trip. Not only is this a must, but it has to be done as soon as possible to prevent corrosion of the mechanical parts – particularly the cooling system and the exhaust – by salt water.

After desalting the engine's cooling system, it is extremely important to rinse the entire machine thoroughly, especially the engine compartment. A pressure washer allows you to reach every part of the hull.

Proper desalting requires a hose and running water. Start first by hose-washing the hull exterior, the storage compartments and, most importantly, the engine compartment. When performing this operation, remember to open the drain holes located at the rear so the water can run out. Next, you should flush the areas where water circulates, ie the engine interior, in particular the cooling system and the exhaust. Without turning on the water, connect the hose to the fitting provided on the engine's cooling system before starting the jet ski's engine and letting it idle. Only then should you turn the water on. This sequence is important and minimises the risk of filling the engine and exhaust with water, which would obviously have severe consequences. When you have finished desalting, shut off the water, empty the exhaust with some revs and finally turn off the engine.

For better results, you can also add a salt-removing product to the running water. This comes in a container that connects directly onto the hose. These products are very effective, but even when using a desalting product, it is always best to desalt immediately. Let the engine run for two or three minutes and rev it up briefly a few times.

Once the engine has been flushed thoroughly, you can use the hose to clean the engine compartment. Remember to open the drain holes so the water drains out, and to run the bilge pump, which will also be desalted as a result. Don't forget the storage compartments, the handlebar and controls, and especially the jet pump. For the latter, you should aim the hose at the entry as well as the exit of the pump. Use a large sponge and pay close attention to the metal parts, particularly the scoop, the ride plate and

the steering nozzle. You should finish the operation by cleaning the exterior – shampooing the hull and the seat, if possible – not forgetting to rinse the trailer or launching cart.

Once desalting is complete, you should rinse out the decanter on the fuel tank vent by opening the lower screw (beware: the water is usually contaminated with fuel), flushing the exhaust with some short, sharp revs (exactly the same as when coming out of the water), and wiping the engine compartment dry by removing any remaining water with a sponge.

↑ To facilitate engine desalting, use of a flushing kit with a blue desalting product is strongly recommended. The kit is simply connected to the hose.

↑ Once opened, the drain plugs let the accumulated water drain out of the hull.

← It is important to let the water drain out completely before closing the engine compartment

Inspection after each outing

AFTER DESALTING, a visual inspection should be made to check the machine's condition. First, check the hull for chips in the gel coat, especially below the waterline. Have a quick look at the waterproofing seals on the storage and engine compartments. Check that the steering moves freely, but without play. On stand-up jet skis, check the state of the handle pole to see if you can find any cracks, which can be caused by wave jumping. Lastly, inspect the jet pump and the impeller for signs of damage caused by rocks, and check the electrical circuit, the most important safety element, especially when riding at sea.

Greasing and lubrication

REGULAR GREASING is essential to prevent corrosion and to ensure good lubrication of moving parts. Follow the instructions in your jet ski's maintenance manual to identify your jet ski's greasing points. They are located on the jet pump housing and make it possible to lubricate the impeller bearings.

Use marine lubricants for routine maintenance of your jet ski.

Protect against condensation

Always leave the engine and storage compartments open (don't forget the fire extinguisher compartment) so they can dry. This precaution is very important and prevents condensation, the greatest enemy of mechanical parts. To do this thoroughly, the seat should be removed – not just left half open – so that the hull interior and the various compartments are well ventilated. Use desalting as an opportunity to inspect the machine and look for possible dents in the hull or any mechanical problems. Obviously, after riding in fresh water, desalting is not required. Nevertheless, it is still preferable to rinse the jet ski with clean water. After coming out of the water, whether desalting or not, always remember to dry your machine following the recommendations mentioned above.

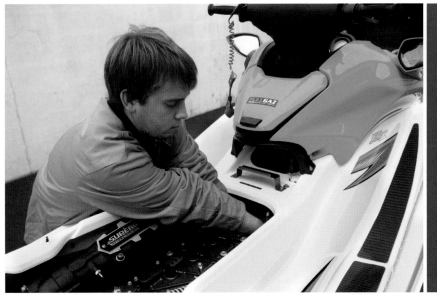

← Lubrication is often neglected because the engine's compartment is difficult to access, But this task is indispensable to the machine's reliability.

↓ Thick oil in a spray can is essential for all lubrication tasks.

A good grease gun is essential and use of high-quality, thick marine grease is required. It is well worth investing in a good-quality product – standard grease offers no water resistance. For the jet pump, remember to lubricate the entire steering assembly, from the steering nozzle joints to the controls located on the handlebar. In the engine compartment, the transmission shaft bearings generally have two or three grease nipples. Take care not to overfill them with grease to avoid damaging or popping out the watertight grease seals: one or two pump strokes are enough for regular maintenance. These grease nipples have rubber protection caps – remember to replace them.

As for the rest, put a little grease on the sensitive spots like exposed hinges and electrical terminals. If you plan to dismantle anything in the engine compartment, put a little marine grease on the screw threads before reinstalling them. Lastly, in order to prevent corrosion on the metal parts – especially on the engine and in the jet pump – you should apply a fine coat of aerosol lubricant to them.

Battery maintenance

A JET SKI BATTERY is special, not least because it can operate in any position and has no vents, thereby eliminating the risk of acid spills in the water. Modern batteries are now frost-resistant and are completely sealed. They do require a specific charger, however, and using one is essential for regular battery maintenance. These chargers are automatic and have many advantages, including the fact that they can be connected directly to the battery's terminals with the battery in place, thus eliminating the need to disconnect and remove it. They also control the charging current automatically and can remain connected for long periods, compensating for energy loss and prolonging the life of the battery. An automatic charger is like insurance for the battery, to keep it in perfect condition and provide maximum power. The latest-generation chargers can identify a battery that is at the end of its life and also allow you to charge a conventional battery. After a trip, if you connect your charger directly to your jet ski's battery, without unscrewing the terminals, you will always be assured of having a battery that is at its best.

In the event of battery failure The lifespan of a battery, especially for the bottom-of-the-range models, is fairly limited. Even with careful maintenance, they rarely last more than three years. It is therefore not unusual to have a battery failure. To avoid this problem, some riders routinely replace their battery after three years. On the shore, it is also tempting to start the jet ski by using jump leads. To do this, you need to take the current from a battery with the same power level: for example, by starting from another jet ski. If you connect to a car battery, particularly one with a large diesel engine, the amperage is far too strong for the electrical circuit and can destroy the jet ski engine's electrics. You should cut the contact with the 'donor' vehicle and disconnect the cables immediately after start-up.

Maintaining your battery is essential to the safety of your ride.

There are some simple rules to follow for new batteries to prolong their lifespan. The first is to follow the start-up protocol strictly, particularly the cooling time, which generally varies from 30 minutes to 1 hour after the first charge. Then – and this is the most important point – it is imperative to charge the battery as normal with an automatic charger so that it delivers all of its power. If you fail to do this, the battery's lifespan will be greatly reduced.

Changing the oil on four stroke engines

FOUR-STROKE ENGINES require an oil change and replacement of the oil filter at least once a year. This must be carried out by suction and not by draining. It is important to have a pump designed specifically for this to suck the old oil out through the dipstick hole. While this operation is quite straightforward, replacement of the oil filter is generally a more delicate task, mainly because of accessibility problems requiring disassembly of the many peripherals around the engine. For this reason, replacement of the oil filter cartridge is often neglected, which can have two consequences: one is that the oil is no longer correctly filtered and the lubrication circuit becomes dirty and clogged; the other is that the filter's metal casing is attacked by corrosion. Inaccessible oil filters holed by rust are the source of some engine failures.

To access the oil filter cartridge and dismantle it, use a special oil filter key sold in motorcycle shops. Note that these oil filters are very exposed to corrosion, so it is important to replace them as indicated in the manufacturer's recommended maintenance programme.

Two-stroke engine maintenance

EVEN THOUGH today almost all modern machines have four-stroke engines, two-stroke engines are still found on most used machines as well as on stand-up competition jet skis marketed by Yamaha and Kawasaki. These simple engines require daily but fairly simple maintenance. The first requirement, which is also undoubtedly the most tiresome, is the need to make your fuel mixture. A two-stroke engine is lubricated only by the oil you add to the petrol. Some old jet skis have an auto-lube system that automatically injects oil into the fuel at a precise rate, which is adjusted according to the engine speed. The stand-up jet skis currently sold do not have such systems, which means you have to make up this oil/fuel mixture for yourself. A special oil designed specifically for two-stroke marine engines is required – using any other oil can wreck the engine.

To make the mix, you need a specific measure, which can still be found in some boat, jet ski or motorcycle shops, and a jerrycan. It is best to use two 10 litre jerrycans (using two lighter 10 litre jerrycans rather than one 20 litre can makes it easier to fill the tank) filled to their correct capacity; then you can add the amount of oil corresponding to the fuel quantity and mix the whole thing by stirring the jerrycans vigorously before filling the jet ski tank. You should not fill the machine's tank with fuel and add the oil afterwards, as the mixture will not be mixed well enough. Likewise, it is preferable to put the oil into the jerrycan first, before putting in the fuel, to facilitate mixing. Preferably, use SP95 unleaded fuel, which is perfectly appropriate for two-stroke engines.

The fuel/oil ratio is usually around 25:1. You should always follow the instructions in the manufacturer's maintenance manual or the oil manufacturer's recommendations. Modern lubricants make it possible to reduce this percentage, but make sure not to overdose the mixture, because not only will this clog the engine and the spark plugs, but it will also cause a lot of exhaust smoke and reduce performance, particularly when revving up.

Apart from this 'daily' obligation of making the mixture at each refill, a two-stroke engine requires little maintenance and does not need oil changes. However, the owner of a two-stroke engine must also keep a spare set of spark plugs on hand and replace them regularly, taking care to use an identical model and also to check the electrode gap (0.7 mm on average). You should also change the spark plugs if you notice an ignition problem.

Even though a two-stroke engine does not require much maintenance, it is still important to replace the piston rings periodically to ensure good performance. Piston ring replacement should be followed by replacement of the pistons, the piston axis, the lower piston rod bearing and the various engine seals, in particular the head gasket. While this is fairly expensive in terms of spare parts, it requires relatively little labour. The two-stroke engines found mainly on stand-up and older jet skis do not have an hour meter, so it can be difficult to determine exactly when to carry out this maintenance task.

Winterisation

WINTERISATION CONSISTS MAINLY of a major clean-up and desalting combined with a thorough greasing of the mechanical parts. The whole idea is to prepare the engine and jet pump for a long period of inactivity and to prevent any risk of corrosion.

Keeping a clean fuel supply

THE FIRST WINTERISATION task is to fill up the fuel tank: filling the tank with fuel limits condensation. But fuel quickly loses its qualities, and it is essential to add a fuel stabiliser/preservative if you

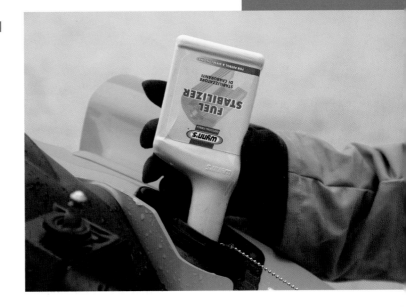

A storage additive is essential to correctly winterise a two- or four-stroke engine.

are going to store your jet ski for longer than two months. This small precaution prevents the formation of deposits in the fuel system that would require disassembly and cleaning when restarting. You can get an additive for fuel storage at jet ski or boat stores and add it to your full tank according to the manufacturer's recommendations. To work properly, the fuel additive must circulate in the engine. You need to run the machine for a few minutes (ideally when desalting) in order to achieve this. When restarting at the end of winter, the fuel and the additive will normally have lost their effectiveness. For two-stroke engines, where oil is mixed with the fuel, it is better to avoid starting the engine with an old mixture, even with an additive. Once again, follow the additive manufacturer's recommendations carefully.

Protecting the engine interior

ONE OF THE MAIN objectives of winterisation is protecting the engine's internal parts from corrosion. To achieve this, the spark plugs must be removed and a fair amount of storage oil should be injected into all of the cylinders. The starter should be activated for a few turns to distribute this oil thoroughly before replacing the spark plugs. Note also that some professionals routinely take compression readings before and after winterisation to check the engine condition. This precaution also makes it possible to check the quality of the winterisation in the event of engine problems when restarting.

While lubrication of the 'upper engine' is essential, with four-stroke engines it is equally desirable to change the oil and replace the oil filter.

Specific lubrication points for winterisation

WHEN WINTERISING, in addition to performing all of the greasing tasks required for routine maintenance, you should also grease some parts of the jet ski to prepare it for storage. For example, in the engine compartment it is advisable to spray storage oil into the engine air intake system by unscrewing the hose clamps and moving the flexible conduits slightly out of the way. While performing this task, you can also check the tightening on all of the hose clamps. Once all the greasing tasks have been completed, you can apply a good coat of aerosol lubricant over the entire engine.

With regards to the jet pump, it is important to thoroughly protect the pump body around the water intake as well as at the outlet nozzle. To do this, use an aerosol grease for motorcycle chains, which has the advantage of being easy to apply and solid enough to adhere well to all of the walls.

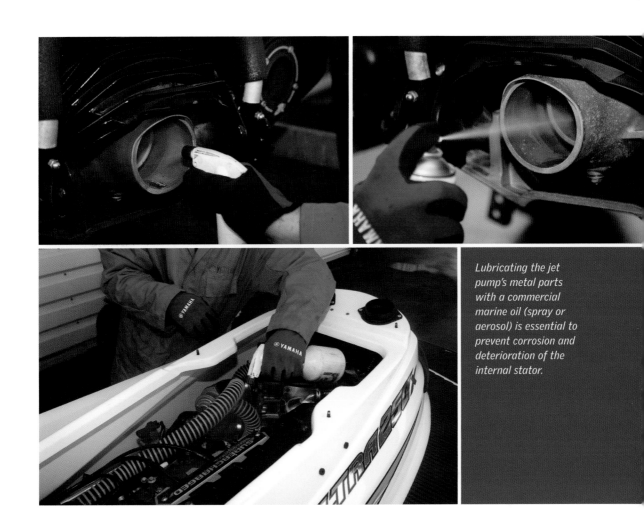

Lubricating the jet pump's metal parts with a commercial marine oil (spray or aerosol) is essential to prevent corrosion and deterioration of the internal stator.

Remember the trailer and protect everything from freezing

WHEN WINTERIZING your jet ski, you also need to maintain its trailer, in particular checking and lubricating the wheel bearings, the hitch and the winch. You should also check the condition and the pressure of the tyres. The jet ski trailer assembly should ideally be stored in a closed garage, away from light and, in particular, be protected from freezing. This precaution is important because it will prevent the residual water in the hitch turning to ice and damaging it. Moreover, condensation should be avoided for engines in winter storage. Ideally, the jet ski should be stored on its trailer in a slightly heated garage. All that's left to do then is to disconnect the battery, check the distilled-water level and put it on charge with an automatic charger for the winter.

Restarting

WHEN RESTARTING, first perform a visual inspection of the jet ski, particularly the engine compartment, exhaust and jet pump, to look for possible traces of corrosion. Theoretically, if winterisation was properly performed, there should be no problem.

The first task involves the battery – checking its level, charging and connecting it, and applying a little grease to the terminals. You should also make sure that the fuel valve is correctly open.

Next, you have to remove all of the spark plugs and activate the starter motor in short bursts to remove the storage oil in the cylinders. Place a rag on the spark plug holes to absorb this oil. Then replace the spark plugs and spark plug leads, checking that they are firmly in place. Also wipe off the excess grease and oil from winterisation.

All that is left to do then is to start the engine, always with short bursts of the starter. Once the engine is running, you can connect the water supply to ensure cooling and let it idle to eliminate the remainder of the storage oil. This operation needs to be carried out in the open air, because with all the excess oil the exhaust will smoke a lot for the first few minutes. Once the engine is turning over normally without smoking, you can close the water to the cooling system and stop the engine. After restarting, the spark plugs should be changed – an essential task for two-stroke engines.

For the first few trips after winterisation it is very important to let the engine warm up gradually and to avoid pushing it too hard. With your first full tank it is best to ride at low speeds to run the engine in.

Jet pump maintenance

JET PUMP MAINTENANCE requires special tools and good technical skills, so if you don't have experience in this field it is better to leave this job to a specialist. The jet pump doesn't require any special service provided it is regularly desalted and winterised before storage. It only needs to be disassembled to replace certain parts, in particular the impeller, the stator, the driveshaft and the bearings. Removing a jet pump doesn't present any great engineering problems. However, disassembling it requires special tools, in particular an extractor for unscrewing the impeller and a grooved spline wrench for holding the transmission shaft. A jet pump cannot be disassembled without these tools, but with them the task can be performed in under an hour.

To perform this task, it is easier to leave the machine on its trailer so you can work at the correct height. You can also remove the jockey wheel to raise the back of the jet ski and immobilise the trailer, which enables you to work more comfortably. Do not try to work on a machine that is moving around. For safety reasons, you must remove the kill switch key to avoid any risk in case of accidental contact with the start button.

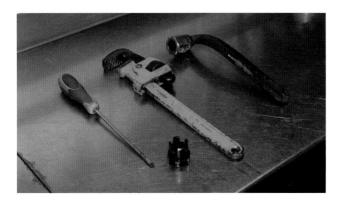

Removing a jet pump is easy enough but requires tools made specifically for your brand of jet ski, especially for removing the impeller. This task requires an extractor to remove the impeller from the transmission shaft and the latter must be immobilised with the aid of a blocking socket. A pipe wrench can be used to remove the extractor. However, this task should be entrusted to a professional.

Dismantling a jet pump begins with the disassembly of all of the steering nozzle controls, in particular the steering rod, but also the trim and reverse, if the machine has them. You should pay close attention to how each part is put together and set them carefully aside in the same order to avoid mistakes. The water circuit hoses should also be removed; then unscrew the four large-diameter bolts securing the fixed nozzle to the body of the jet pump. As this assembly is put together with joint compound, it is not unusual to encounter some resistance when removing it. If this happens, locate the two notches on each side designed to fit a small screwdriver and lever it off. Be careful, as there isn't much room around the

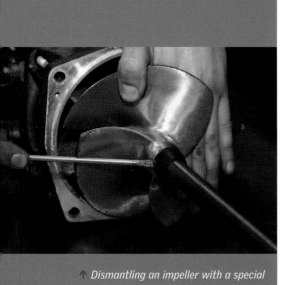

↑ Dismantling an impeller with a special extractor. Note that its nut is protected by a rubber seal, which must be carefully removed using a screwdriver.

↓ To remove an impeller, block the transmission shaft with an appropriate tool, like a hexagonal socket spanner held in a vice.

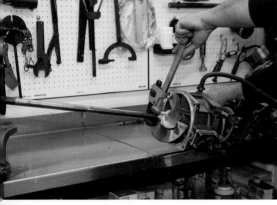

↑ Removing the extractor.

pump. When it has been separated, the body of the pump can be removed complete with the driveshaft.

After removing the pump, it is best to lay it out on a workbench to disassemble it. First, check the condition of the bearings. The transmission shaft should turn freely without any hard spots and there should not be any play. Also check the condition of the shaft, which should not show any significant signs of wear.

For the disassembly itself, remove the rubber that protects the impeller nut with the aid of a screwdriver tip. You need to handle this part carefully, taking care not to damage it – its role is to prevent water from entering the driveshaft thread.

Once it is released, all you have to do is unscrew the impeller using a special socket that fits over the transmission shaft, while holding the shaft with a suitable tool that is placed on the shaft grooves and is held in a vice. Holding the transmission shaft directly in the vice is likely to mark it and make it unusable. Once the impeller is free, the only thing left to do is to extract it. The pump is now disassembled and you can check its condition.

Checking the jet pump

THE MAIN PARTS that make up the jet pump are the impeller and the stator. It is important to check both of these parts at the same time and not just examine the impeller. For optimum output, these two parts must be paired, exactly like the cylinder/ piston assembly in an engine. There must be a small clearance between them, in accordance with the manufacturer's recommendations. With both parts placed horizontally and turning freely, the clearance between the outside of the impeller and the stator is measured with a feeler gauge. Each manufacturer specifies the recommended clearance in their shop manuals (generally 0.50mm), as well as the service limit measurement (0.90mm). When this limit is

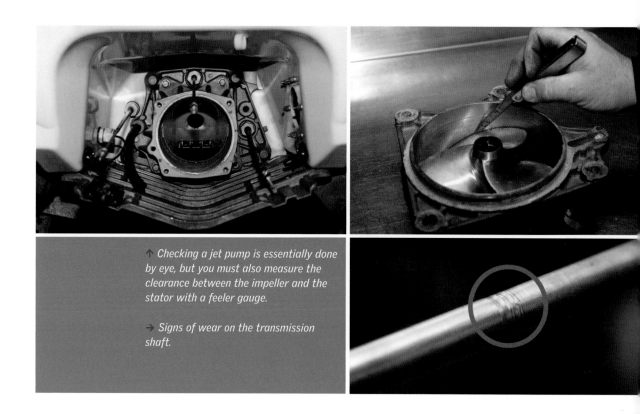

↑ *Checking a jet pump is essentially done by eye, but you must also measure the clearance between the impeller and the stator with a feeler gauge.*

→ *Signs of wear on the transmission shaft.*

reached, the stator must be replaced, even when it has no apparent signs of wear. A stator can simply wear out, but more often it is made unusable by damage from stones sucked into the pump. Poor desalting followed by prolonged storage can also cause significant oxidation of the stator surface. This is called 'swelling'. If such corrosion is superficial and localised, it can be mechanically eliminated as a makeshift repair.

Impeller repair

DESPITE BEING made of stainless steel, the impeller is still the pump's most vulnerable part. It can't avoid being struck by stones sucked into the pump. Having said that, in some cases an impeller can be repaired. For this to be possible, it should be neither misshapen nor too chipped. Some marks on a blade's leading edge can be fixed with a flat file, primarily to eliminate small burs. Some pros also use disc grinders for this job. To perform this operation correctly, you must have a gauge for checking the impeller's pitch, especially for models with variable or progressive pitch. Some users repair their impeller once or twice a year to prolong its performance. It should be noted that it is also possible to rebuild a jet ski

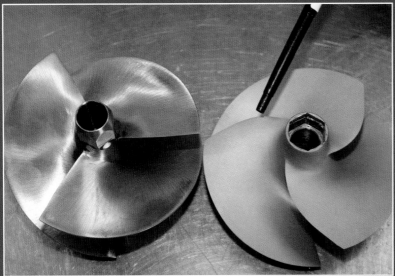

← The leading edges of the impeller have to be in good condition. In this photo (above) the damage is irreparable.

↑ An impeller can be repaired by using a file to remove small marks caused by contact with stones.
→ Some professionals use a small grinder for this operation.

↑ Repairing an impeller with a file.

impeller, but this should really be done primarily by specialists. One of the few ways to modify a jet ski's performance is by changing the characteristics of its impeller. Changing the impeller model makes it possible to obtain more acceleration or a higher top speed, for example, enabling you to tune the machine according to its use. The impeller is open to compromise and its basic elements are universal. For this reason, when replacing it, you should not hesitate to choose the most appropriate impeller for your use. Some old jet skis on the second-hand market still have a low-performance aluminium impeller. Replacing this with a stainless steel model is not difficult.

Checking the inclination of the blades with a pitch gauge.

Cleaning the cooling system filter

MOST JET SKIS have an open cooling system, ie the engine is cooled by water taken in by the jet pump, which is then expelled through the exhaust. This is why you have to desalt the engine with fresh water after each use at sea. When dismantling the jet pump, it is possible to clean the filter located at the cooling circuit entry, which is designed to prevent the intrusion of small stones. To do this, all you have to do is remove the small aluminium casing held by four screws and then remove the synthetic filter to clean it. On reassembly, take care to place the various parts back facing the right way, and put a little sealing compound on the mating surfaces.

A filter at the cooling circuit entry prevents clogging of the system. Nevertheless, it is essential to periodically clean these easy-to-access filters once the pump is dismantled. A simple hexagonal socket spanner is generally used for this job.

Impeller and pump reassembly

REASSEMBLY is carried out by reversing the disassembly process.
It is not necessary to apply a lot of torque when tightening the
impeller, as the rotation of the impeller shaft has a self-tightening
effect. You must not use 'thread lockers', like Loctite adhesive, or the next
disassembly could prove to be very difficult. Next, you need to clean the
pump's mating surfaces, as well as its mount, with a soft brass brush.
Then apply a sealing compound to the pump body before remounting it. It
is also worth considering greasing the driveshaft grooves. Finally, tighten
the pump body and reassemble the nozzle controls before checking that
the steering operates properly.

Before remounting a jet pump, it is essential to clean the mating surfaces with a cutter or a very soft brass brush dipped in some solvent, and to apply a new bead of sealing compound.

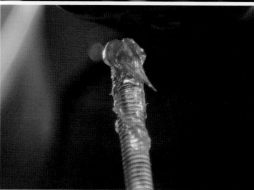

↑ *Even though lubrication of a mechanical trim control is within the ability of every jet ski user, it is often neglected.*

→ *To grease the handlebar, unscrew its end and remove the trim handle.*

Trim control maintenance

SOME MACHINES have a trim control system which makes it possible to adjust the angle of the nozzle and thus to modify the machine's plane. The trim control can be electric, as on certain Sea-Doo models, or mechanically cable driven, in particular on Yamaha machines. Kawasaki does not offer this facility on production models. A mechanical control requires regular lubrication. For this simple operation it is sufficient to dismantle the control at the handlebar and, using a brush, apply a little grease on the slide and on the cables before reassembling the whole thing, remembering also to lubricate the screws. Note that the mechanism has a ball and a spring. Take care when disassembling not to lose them and check that they are in place when reassembling.

→ *Greasing the trim cables and the winder generously will guarantee optimal trim function. Don't forget to grease the cable in the sheath.*

Sea-Doo – specific maintenance

WHILE THE JAPANESE manufacturers Kawasaki and Yamaha offer generally similar technologies for the UK and French markets, the Canadian manufacturer Sea-Doo uses some unique, proprietary technology, which requires special maintenance. The latest Sea-Doo models are distinguished by having a cooling system that is not open like those of its rivals, but closed like those of terrestrial motor vehicles. Another unique feature of the Sea-Doo is its jet pump design, which on some of its machines has a synthetic sleeve or wear ring.

The closed-circuit cooling system

WITH THE SEA-DOO system, water is replaced by a coolant, which circulates in the engine and in the ride plate, making it act like a heat exchanger, ie a radiator. This system makes a difference for machines used intensively at sea by avoiding the circulation of salt water in the engine. It is therefore important to check the coolant level in the expansion tank, exactly as on a car or motorbike. The level varies with the rise in engine temperature and has to be between the two reference marks on the bowl. You should take care not to exceed the maximum

Sea-Doo jet skis have a closed cooling system, like that found on a car or a motorcycle, thus avoiding the circulation of salt water in the engine interior. It is best to use a coolant made specifically for an aluminium engine as it is less corrosive than water and prevents the risk of freezing in winter.

level and also not to open the cap while the engine is running or when it is hot. After refilling, check that the cap is correctly in place and that it is locked by tightening it to the second notch. The coolant is standard and is identical to the one used by cars and motorcycles, but you should always choose a high-quality product that contains good anti-corrosion agents. In order to prevent corrosion problems, avoid topping up with tap water or even with distilled water. Note also that sometimes the original coolant is unsuitable for use in very high temperatures, especially in warm seas and in the tropics. Sea-Doo recommends replacing the coolant every two years in order to maintain its properties.

Desalting a Sea-Doo system

THE CLOSED cooling system only simplifies the desalting operation a little, because the exhaust is still cooled by the water in which the jet ski is operating and therefore needs to be rinsed with a flow of fresh water. To facilitate this task, it is best to mount a snap-on coupling, like the ones manufactured by Gardena, directly onto the water inlet located at the back of the machine in the jet pump housing. As when desalting a 'conventional' jet ski, to avoid filling the exhaust and the engine with water you must first start the engine, then turn on the water. You should avoid running the engine for too long – no more than five to seven minutes is really necessary – not only because cooling on land is not as effective as when the machine is in the water, but also because of another peculiarity of Sea-Doo jet skis, which is that they have a carbon seal on the transmission shaft, which is also prone to overheating when out of the water. Also worth noting is that since the ride plate acts as a radiator, it is essential to treat it with care, particularly when transporting the machine. You should be careful, for example, not to let the jet ski and trailer tip backwards when launching or hauling out, as hitting the ground could easily damage this 'radiator' and cause a cooling problem.

Jet pump stator with wear ring

THIS TECHNOLOGY has two noteworthy advantages: it prevents corrosion problems and reduces jet pump maintenance costs, since the wear ring costs significantly less than purchasing a new alloy stator. Having said that, this synthetic part wears faster and is less resistant to

Dismantling and maintaining a Sea-Doo jet pump is a quick and easy task.

← *Removing a Sea-Doo jet pump's impeller is simple, even though this job requires a few special tools, notably to hold the transmission shaft.*

sand and stones passing through the jet pump. It is therefore important to check the condition of this part regularly. A wear ring or stator that is too scratched can cause the complex phenomenon of cavitation, which results in considerably reduced jet pump output and thus a reduction in the jet ski's performance. Cavitation also causes faster deterioration of moving parts, particularly the impeller. The Sea-Doo jet pump design is fairly simple and allows for fast dismantling while following the protocol for a standard jet pump. The big difference lies in the stator, which is composed of one alloy piece rather than two, but with a wear ring at the impeller location. This wear ring is simply force-pressed into its housing. After removing the pump body, a visual inspection can be carried out easily.

A unique feature of the Sea-Doo jet pump is that it has a synthetic stator (wear ring) which, although it wears out faster than an alloy one, can be easily replaced.

→ (Top) An unusable Sea-Doo stator.

→ To remove the wear ring you have to hold it in a vice and extract it by hitting the edges of the pump exterior with a nylon mallet. The new wear ring can be installed with a hydraulic press or by putting a solid wooden block on it and hitting it with a sharp, perfectly placed blow.

To replace the wear ring, you have to remove the jet pump cone, which does not pose any problem. Check the watertightness of the O-rings by looking for any traces of water. Next, the impeller is removed, which requires a special extractor. Once the stator is removed, all that's left is to extract the old wear ring by holding it in a vice and hitting the stator with a mallet. You must take care not to hit the stator's fragile parts, in particular the mating planes and the thin protruding pieces. This method is the fastest but there's a bit of a knack to it; the other method consists of cutting the ring at several points on its circumference with a small power saw, taking special care not to damage the stator.

To install the new wear ring, you need to place the stator on a flat surface on a bench and use a large wooden block and a hammer. You'll need to identify the right place to position the new wear ring, then use some sharp, well-placed blows to install it. Always check that the wear ring has gone into its housing perfectly. Using this simple method you can make do without a hydraulic press.

Inspection and reassembly

BEFORE REASSEMBLING the jet pump, you have to check the condition of the nozzle in several places. On the fixed part, especially if the jet pump has sucked up some stones, you must check the state of the two water inlets located inside the nozzle. These two small protruding tubes play the role of an automatic bilge pump by using the pump flow to suck water out of the hull. If broken, they don't perform this function anymore and allow water to enter the hull. Apart from this, it is important to check for the presence of the reverse gate spring, the state of the seals, the two parts of the pump assembly, and the nozzle assembly. Lastly, note that the Sea-Doo jet pump is reassembled without joint compound.

↓ *Before final reassembly of a Sea-Doo jet pump, you must check the condition of the seals, the bilge pump outlets and the reverse gate spring.*

Towing a Sea-Doo
The Sea-Doo jet pump design also limits towing in the water. Without the engine, the Sea-Doo bilge pump system allows water to get into the hull.

Hull repairs

BECAUSE IT IS MADE OF composite materials, a jet ski has the enormous advantage of being easy to repair, at least the non-structural parts of the hull or deck. Small knocks are practically inevitable when using the machine – obviously when riding, but especially during landing, transportation and storage. In this section we will look at common repairs for these small dents. Larger repairs – especially on double-bottomed hulls – should be reserved for professionals, as they require technical knowledge. While some dealers have a workshop where they can carry out fibreglassing and repair damaged machines, others subcontract this work to specialists.

Hull repairs require some skill, and common products are readily available at chandleries.

Repairing a chip in the gel coat

THE GEL COAT is a layer of high-quality resin applied on top of a composite material. It has several advantages, one of which is to give the fibreglass a beautiful, opaque and smooth finish. A superficial chip in the gel coat is both very common and easy to mend. However, the final paint touch-up is difficult to do properly and discreetly, especially on coloured hulls. Hulls painted white at least have the advantage of making minor repairs almost invisible and of eliminating the need for a paint touch-up.

Repairing a chip is a simple task and it is always better to get it done quickly. Gel coat resin is readily available in small quantities, usually in chandleries. You should follow the manufacturer's recommendations for application and drying times. Gel coat is applied directly with a brush. You should clean the chipped area with a little fine sandpaper beforehand, then apply several thin layers before sanding the whole thing with a very fine-grain water sandpaper to

A small chip in the gel coat is easily repaired, especially on white hulls. Marine paint, a brush and polish are all that are needed in this case.

obtain a beautiful finish. To remove any traces of sanding you should finish the job with an abrasive car polish. With a few minutes of work and a few hours of drying, a chip in the gel coat can be effectively repaired.

Fibreglass repairs

OUR REPAIR EXAMPLE is illustrated by a Yamaha jet ski which has suffered a minor blow to the deck (1). Its repair, however, is made complex by its location across several ridges (2). The first step consists of removing the bumper and the rub rail and then carefully marking quite a broad working area with a felt pen. Then, using a pneumatic file, the fibre is exposed over the whole of this area (3). Finishing is done by hand with medium-grain sandpaper (4). At this stage, the site of the blow is almost invisible, hence the importance of marking the area to be repaired beforehand (5).

The first stage consists of removing the gel coat with a pneumatic file, after marking the area to be repaired. You have to measure the area to cut the cloth 'patches'.

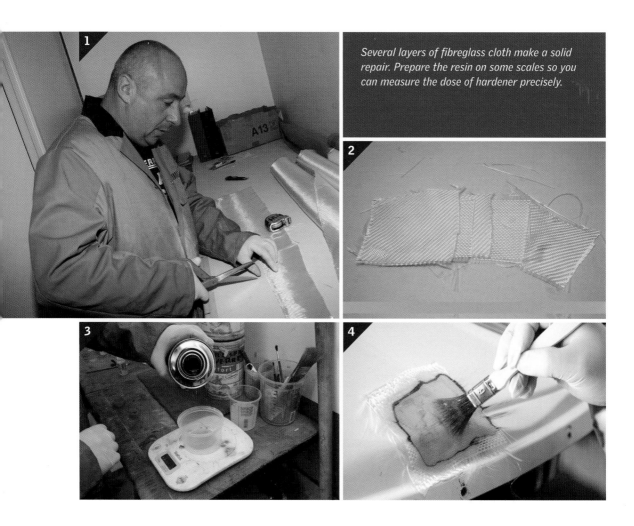

Several layers of fibreglass cloth make a solid repair. Prepare the resin on some scales so you can measure the dose of hardener precisely.

Next, you need to cut several pieces of roving (1), which is a fabric of woven glass fibres (2), after you have taken precise measurements of the area to be repaired. In this case, five pieces of roving with different weaves will be used. This detail ensures better repair strength and also allows you to build up the right thickness of fibre. Once the 'patches' are cut out, you need to prepare the resin by adding the correct proportion of hardener to it (3). This job is usually done on scales to get the perfect mix; if not done properly, the resin will quickly become unusable because of too much hardener, or else it will be too runny to apply, particularly for vertical applications. It should be noted that both polyester and epoxy resins are available, the former offering the advantage of drying much more quickly, although in theory it is not as strong.

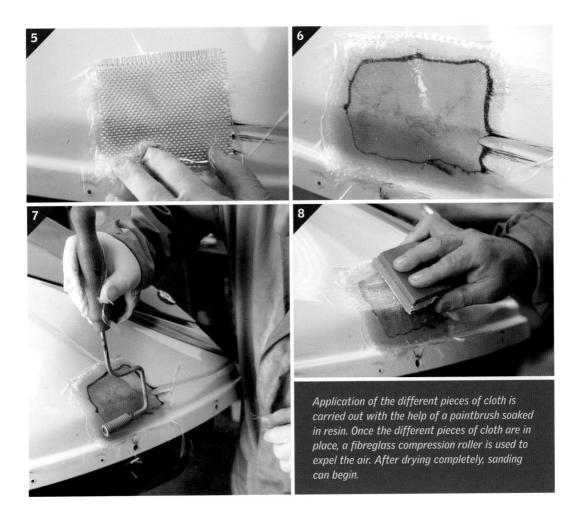

Application of the different pieces of cloth is carried out with the help of a paintbrush soaked in resin. Once the different pieces of cloth are in place, a fibreglass compression roller is used to expel the air. After drying completely, sanding can begin.

Once the resin is prepared and mixed, you have to work quickly. Wearing gloves, start by applying a layer of resin (4), then a piece of cloth (5), then another layer of resin. It is important that each piece of cloth is perfectly soaked and correctly positioned on the area. You have to repeat the operation until the five patches have been applied (6). Once the fabric is laid, you then need to use the fibreglass compression roller, which, as its name suggests, removes the air between the various layers of fabric (7). This will ensure the 'patch' is perfectly fixed before being left to dry in accordance with the resin manufacturer's instructions. The ends of the various pieces of fabric remain visible and will be removed automatically when sanding after the drying phase (8).

Sanding is done by hand to enable you to follow the repair contours closely. The pneumatic file is only used very locally (1). With coarse-grain sandpaper the resin is sanded quickly and easily. Even though sanding is both tiresome and dirty, as it generates a fair amount of dust, it doesn't take too long. It is advisable to wear a dust mask and glasses. At this stage, the repair can be said to be almost complete (2).

All that remains is to putty the area (3) and to sand again, but with a finer-grained sandpaper to get a beautifully finished repair area. The plastic putty used for our repair is also readily available from professionals who work in fibreglass.

After puttying and sanding (4), the repaired area is then primed. When doing this you should protect the jet ski from the spray mist with paper and masking tape (5). There are primers of

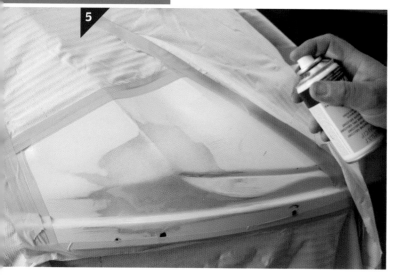

A paint touch-up done by a professional guarantees a beautiful finish after a repair.

various qualities, including coloured primers. For our repair, we used a primer especially designed for boat hulls that provides a beautiful finish (6). However, our Yamaha jet ski was still then sent to an automotive body shop to receive a final coat of paint applied in a dust-free spray booth and heat-dried. This job, which is usually subcontracted to the automotive repair pros, was completed in two days and the result was impeccable (7). All that remained for us to do was to replace the side protections and to change the bumper bar, which was destroyed in the collision. The overall cost of this fibreglass repair was around 350 euros.

7

SPORT AND RECREATION

WHILE RIDING A JET SKI IS PRIMARILY A FORM OF RECREATION, IT IS ALSO A SPORT AND CAN TAKE SEVERAL FORMS. The Jet Sport Racing Association of Great Britain governs jet ski competitions in this country.

Freeride

FREERIDE IS THE NEWEST jet ski discipline; it is also the most spectacular and continues to grow in popularity. It began in the middle of the 1990s with the increase in jet ski power, when riders found themselves in surfing spots for wave-jumping sessions. These riders developed techniques to execute various jumps and these quickly grew in complexity. They also worked hard on the development of their machines, particularly to get power at low revs to facilitate the increase in speed before the jumps, and also to modify the hulls and the decks. The UK is well represented in this discipline and the number of talented riders continues to grow.

↑ *Jet ski development has benefited greatly from the manufacturers' involvement in jet ski competitions.*

↓ *Freeride is performed at sea. This practice was born in the middle of the 90s. With its free spirit and beautiful locations, freeride is very much like surfing, even though the primary objective remains, above all, wave jumping.*

The backflip is the classic freeride trick. Some riders can even perform a double backflip.

Above all, freeride represents free spirit, and this young sport is still practised largely by amateurs.

The principle of freeride is obviously to use the wave. Each rider knows his own location extremely well.

← Freeride jet skis are specially equipped for the sport, notably with holds for the hands and feet.

← Freeride is practised in rapids and in many wild environments, especially in the United States.

→ Freeride is essentially, but not exclusively, performed on stand-up jet skis.

↓ Freestyle involves performing the maximum number of tricks in two minutes. Each rider is scored by a jury.

Freestyle

FREESTYLE WAS ONE OF THE FIRST jet ski disciplines and, like freeride, consists of performing tricks, but in sheltered waters rather than at sea, and within a two-minute time limit. In recent years, professional riders have developed very impressive tricks such as the backflip, which is reserved for the elite. However, every stand-up jet ski rider can test themselves in freestyle with tricks that are simple but that require some specialist technique.

As well as the tricks, speed and follow-through are very important to get the best marks from the jury.

← The most impressive stunt is still the loop. The best competitors perform two loops in a row.

↓ The fountain is one of the basic freestyle tricks and can be performed by amateurs.

Some freestyle tricks

▶ **The fountain:** *The rider uses his machine's jet to make a geyser.*

▶ **The submarine:** *The rider takes off and dives into the water with the machine before resurfacing.*

▶ **The candle:** *The rider sets his machine near vertical in the water and runs with it there to keep it from falling backwards.*

↑ The backflip, a trick reserved for experts.

Rally raids

ALSO KNOWN as cross-country rallies, rally raids are run at sea, over several stages, and demand good navigation skills as well as very good physical condition, especially in rough seas. Offshore rally raids require an assistance team for supplies. The world championship is held every year at the end of June at Oléron, France.

Speed and endurance

RACES ON closed courses are the most accessible. They are generally run on inland waters in several 15–20 minute stages. Endurance races are run on the same courses over several hours or several laps.

Competing

THE JSRA, affiliated to the IJSBA (the International Jet Sport Boating Association from where it takes its class rules) and the Royal Yachting Association's Powerboat Racing division, is the UK's only recognised body for jet sport racing. With the affiliation to the RYA the JSRA receives comprehensive event and public liability insurance cover and the complete support of this powerful institution.

The JSRA site has comprehensive information regarding what is needed to enter competitions. Briefly these entail:

- **RYA licence** *(medical required)*
- **JSRA membership licence**
- **Completed race entry form**
- **Entry fee**
- **All new participants** *will be required to sit a one-off short 20-question induction test based on racing health and safety requirements*

In addition there may be site-specific requirements at some events – these are generally communicated in advance via the JSRA website and newsletters.

All competitors must sign in prior to the competition and anyone under the age of 18 must also be signed in by a parent/guardian.

Stand-up jet skiing is still the most spectacular of the jet ski sports, even if the performance of stand-ups is not comparable to that of runabout models.

Manufacturers sometimes invest large sums in runabout races to promote their products.

Mandatory equipment for competitors

BELOW is a list of mandatory equipment for competitors. In addition, gloves and goggles are highly recommended.

Ski riders

- ▶ **Wetsuit or drysuit** *(no shorts)*
- ▶ **Back protector** *(motorcycle style)*
- ▶ **Approved** *flotation device*
- ▶ **Approved** *safety helmet*
- ▶ **Footwear** *(laces must be taped for freestyle)*

Runabout and Sport Riders

- ▶ **Wetsuit or drysuit** *(no shorts)*
- ▶ **Back protector** *(motorcycle style)*
- ▶ **Approved** *flotation device*
- ▶ **Approved** *safety helmet*
- ▶ **Footwear**
- ▶ **Approved upper thigh guards** *and lower leg protection*

While it is not mandatory for freestyle competitors to wear a back protector, shin guards or a safety helmet, it is recommended that this equipment is worn when practising.

All competitors must also carry a fire extinguisher – minimum of 4kg.

The power of factory-sponsored machines is impressive. They sometimes exceed 400hp and have special hulls.

Lake Havasu:
The jet ski Mecca

EVERY YEAR, the World Jet Ski Championship is held in the United States on the edges of the Colorado river at Lake Havasu, Arizona. For one week, this small, quiet town is transformed into a nautical stadium and welcomes the best riders in the world for closed-course races and freestyle competitions. An open-air expo is also organised.

The world championship races, on the edges of the Colorado river. The simultaneous starts are the most impressive.

↑ The organisation of
closed-course races is
much like motocross, with
a simultaneous start and a
highly coveted first turn.

← The power of some jet
skis now exceeds 260hp,
which requires considerable
skill to handle but also
provides countless thrills.

'Adventure' raids

JET SKI RIDING can also take the form of adventure raids. Organised across the world, these raids last for several days and are held in Africa, South America, the Caribbean and Scandinavia. Some particularly well-organised raids are within the capability of all experience levels. Moreover, the jet skis are generally available on site. Although expensive, these raids are turnkey and very accessible. They are a real adventure and make it possible to ride a jet ski in a variety of unique landscapes.

↑ The jet ski is a tool for both adventure and discovery made accessible to all through raids organised worldwide. As a rule, the machine is provided by the organiser, and the participant only has to get on the plane with their jet ski equipment!

Acknowledgements from the original French edition

The production of this jet ski guide has only been possible with the support and participation of many people working in the jet ski world. Thanks go to all those who give their time and knowledge to make this world accessible to all ...

First and foremost, I must thank the professionals who opened the doors of their workshops to us and devoted entire days to the creation of the technical section. A big thanks to Pierre Helluin and Muriel Aufrère, as well as all the Pierrot Tech team.

Also, this guide would not have been possible without Philippe Ducloy of Jet 7, nor without his team and notably Hervé Turquet and Nicolas Moy. A big thanks also to the nautical professionals who facilitated access to information regarding practice, training and regulations, and especially to Gérard Ouvrard from Paris Nautique (www.paris-nautique.com).

I must also thank those responsible for communications at the French importers and notably Grégory Derlon of BRP France and Chrystelle Gry of Yamaha Motors France, who contributed enormously to this guide.

A big thank you also to the riders who first opened the way for jet ski riding in France, notably Michel Muller and René Robin, without whom the jet ski would not have enjoyed such success in our country.

Finally, thanks to all the jet ski specialists in France, whether they are opinion leaders, journalists, riders or users, for their precious help: Denis Derrien and Alain Boissy of aquariders.net; Christine and Jérôme Bolla of Fun Jet Magazine; Thierry Scharff of Hydrojet Magazine; Jean Chignac; François Regis; Anne Leprince; Vincent Thill; and the Runavanti brothers.

Photo credits

Yamaha Motors France
Kawasaki
Sea-Doo
Ludovic Mouveau
The author's archives

Index